C# 13 Programming Essentials

.NET 9 Edition

C# 13 Programming Essentials - .NET 9 Edition

ISBN-13: 978-1-965764-02-2

Rev: 1.0

https://www.payloadbooks.com

Contents

Table of Contents

Chapter 1

1. Start Here

This book is a comprehensive guide to mastering the C# 13 programming language and the .NET 9 SDK, providing a thorough learning experience for both beginners and experienced developers. With 31 detailed chapters, 30 online knowledge quizzes, and access to downloadable project code, this guide is structured to support your journey from basic concepts to advanced programming techniques, all within the Visual Studio Code environment.

We will start by introducing the foundational components of the C# ecosystem, providing an overview of the Common Language Infrastructure (CLI), the Common Intermediate Language (CIL), and the Virtual Execution System (VES). These initial sections will offer a deeper understanding of the platform's architecture. Following that, we will provide step-by-step instructions for installing and using the Visual Studio Code environment.

As you advance, you will learn about the foundational principles of the C# language. This will include exploring topics such as variables, constants, operators, flow control, and loops. These basic concepts will then be expanded to cover object-oriented programming (OOP), with an emphasis on inheritance, abstract classes, interfaces, and structures.

Beyond the basics, this book advances into more specialized areas, including string manipulation, working with arrays and collections, handling exceptions, and implementing asynchronous programming techniques. These sections are designed to deepen your understanding and equip you with the skills necessary to build more sophisticated apps.

Whether you are new to programming or seeking to refine your skills, *C# 13 Programming Essentials - .NET 9 Edition* offers the knowledge and practical guidance you need to succeed in C# development.

1.1 Source code download

The source code and Visual Studio Code project files for the examples contained in this book can be downloaded using the following link:

https://www.payloadbooks.com/product/csharp13/

After downloading and unzipping the file, you will find the projects in the "C# Essentials" workspace folder. In Visual Studio Code, you can open the workspace by selecting *File -> Open Folder...* from the menu bar, navigating to the workspace folder, and clicking Open to load the projects.

1.2 Feedback

We want you to be satisfied with your purchase of this book. Therefore, if you find any errors in the book or have any comments, questions, or concerns, please contact us at *info@payloadbooks.com*.

1.3 Errata

While we make every effort to ensure the accuracy of the content of this book, inevitably, a book covering a subject area of this size and complexity may include some errors and oversights. Any known issues with the book will be outlined, together with solutions, at the following URL:

https://www.payloadbooks.com/csharp13-errata/

If you find an error not listed in the errata, please email our technical support team at *info@payloadbooks.com*.

1.4 Download the color eBook

Thank you for purchasing the print edition of this book. Your purchase includes a color copy of the book in PDF format.

If you would like to download the PDF version of this book, please email proof of purchase (for example, a receipt, delivery notice, or photo of the physical book) to *info@payloadbooks.com*, and we will provide you with a download link.

1.5 Take the knowledge tests

Look for this section at the end of most chapters and use the link or scan the QR code to take a knowledge quiz to test and reinforce your understanding of the covered topic. Use the following link to review the full list of tests available for this book:

https://www.answertopia.com/4my3

Chapter 2

2. The History of Programming Languages and C#

C# is part of the never-ending quest to make programming computers as easy and efficient as possible for humans. While it is easy to describe C# as another object-oriented programming language, the fact is that C# is an integral part of an entire development and execution infrastructure. The primary object of these initial chapters is to provide an overview of both the C# language and the infrastructure on which it relies.

2.1 The history of programming languages

The problem with programming is that computers think exclusively in numbers (0 and 1, to be precise), known as machine code, while humans communicate using words. In the early days, programmers entered machine code directly into computers to program them. This, as you can imagine, was a laborious and error-prone process. The next evolution was associating brief human-readable commands with the corresponding machine code. For example, a programmer could enter the command MOV to transfer a value from one microprocessor register to another. These commands would then be translated into machine code by a piece of software called an assembler, thereby giving this command syntax the name Assembly Language.

Next came a series of high-level languages designed to make it easier for humans to write programs. These programs are written using a human-readable syntax and then either compiled to machine code by a compiler or interpreted by an interpreter on the processor's behalf. Such languages include BASIC, COBOL, Pascal, and Fortran. Another language is C, which was created at AT&T Bell Labs in the late 1960s and early 1970s. Then, in the late 1970s and early 1980s, work started on an object-oriented approach to C programming, culminating in a new, object-oriented variant of C known as C++.

The story, however, continues. The problem with C++ was that it was too easy to make programming mistakes. For example, C++ would quite happily allow a programmer to make coding mistakes that would cause buffers to overflow, memory locations to be arbitrarily overwritten, and introduce memory leaks that would cause applications to bloat to the point of using up the entire physical memory and swap space on a system. Another problem encountered with C, C++, and all other compiled languages is that the source code must be recompiled for each processor type, making it difficult to port an application from one hardware platform to another.

To address the shortcomings of C and C++, Sun Microsystems started work on a new programming language and execution environment in the 1990s. The result was called Java. Java consists of a programming language with many of the pitfalls of C++ removed, a portable intermediate byte code format, a runtime environment (called the virtual machine) that executes the byte code and handles issues such as memory management, and a vast suite of libraries providing all the functionality required to develop enterprise-class applications (such as networking, file handling, database access, graphics, etc.).

Java gained rapid acceptance, and for a time, Microsoft began its Java "embrace and extend" campaign. Sun was happy for Microsoft to embrace Java but reached for their lawyers when they realized that the "extend" part was a plan for Microsoft to introduce their own proprietary version of the language. Politics ensued, and Microsoft eventually walked away from Java. Soon after, Microsoft started talking about something called .NET, followed by a programming language called C#.

2.2 What exactly is C#?

"What does all this history have to do with C#?" I hear you ask. The origins of the C# programming syntax can be traced back to C and C++. If you are already familiar with C or C++ (or even Kotlin or Swift, for that matter), then you have a big head start in learning C#. The same can be said of syntax similarities between Java, C, C++, and C# syntax. In addition, C# also inherits many of the benefits of Java in terms of memory handling (better known as garbage collection) and an intermediate byte code that negates the need to recompile an application for each target hardware platform. C# is also accompanied by a vast framework of libraries designed to provide the programmer with ready-made solutions to almost every imaginable scenario.

Despite these similarities, there are differences between the Java and C# infrastructures. Therefore, the next chapter will provide an overview of the C# infrastructure.

2.3 Who is using C#?

Although some significant new programming languages have been released since the introduction of C# (such as Swift and Kotlin), C# is still evolving as a language and has a vast and growing user base.

At the time of writing, for example, C# was ranked on the TIOBE Index in 5th place among the top 50 most widely used programming languages (eclipsed only by C, Java, Python, and C++).

C# is used to develop desktop, mobile, and server applications, as well as web-based applications and services. It is the programming language of choice on all Microsoft platforms and is used to program within the Unity Real-Time Development Platform.

2.4 Take the knowledge test

Click the link below or scan the QR code to test your knowledge and understanding of the history of C#:

https://www.answertopia.com/qoe2

2.5 Summary

C# is a programming language created by Microsoft that combines elements from other popular languages like C, C++, and Java. It's designed to make programming simpler and more efficient with features like memory management to reduce errors and intermediate byte code for compatibility across platforms. C# is used for desktop, mobile, server, web, and game development and is among the top 10 most widely used programming languages.

Chapter 3

3. C# Infrastructure

This chapter will introduce the infrastructure on which the C# language is built. By the end of the chapter, you will have a clear understanding of what acronyms such as CLI, CLR, VES, JIT, and .NET mean.

3.1 The Common Language Infrastructure (CLI)

C# is an object-oriented programming language. It is essentially a standard defining what constitutes valid syntax. On its own, C# is of little use because it depends upon the Common Language Infrastructure (CLI) for the compilation and execution of applications. The CLI, in turn, is a standard that defines specifications for the following components:

- Virtual Execution System (VES)
- Common Intermediate Language (CIL)
- Common Type System (CTS)
- Common Language Specification (CLS)
- Framework

In the remainder of this chapter, we will examine each CLI component to understand how the CLI environment fits together.

3.2 Common Intermediate Language (CIL)

Unlike the C and C++ compilers, which compile the source code to machine code understood by the target microprocessor, the C# compiler compiles to an intermediate byte code format known as the Common Intermediate Language (CIL). This code can be executed on any system with a CLI-compliant Virtual Execution System (VES). Therefore, there is no need to compile an application for every target platform.

The word "Common" in Common Intermediate Language is used because this format is common to more than just the C# programming language. In fact, any programming language may target the CIL, allowing libraries and code modules from different languages to execute together in the same application. Typical languages for which CIL compilation is available include Visual Basic, COBOL, PowerShell, Python, and C++.

3.3 Virtual Execution System (VES)

The VES (referred to as the *runtime*) is the environment in which the CIL byte code is executed. The VES reads the byte code generated by the C# compiler and uses a Just in Time (JIT) compiler to compile the byte code down to the native machine code of the processor on which it is running. While executing, this code does so in conjunction with a runtime agent, which manages the execution process. As a result, this executing code is known as *managed code*, and the process handles issues such as *garbage collection* (to handle memory allocation and de-allocation), memory access, and type safety to ensure that the code does not do anything it is not supposed to do.

A term often used in connection with the VES is the Common Language Runtime (CLR). The CLR is officially the name given to Microsoft's implementation of the VES component of the CLI specification.

It is worth noting that the JIT process can introduce a startup delay in the execution of an application. One option available with .NET to avoid this problem is pre-compiling CLI byte code to native machine code using the NGen compiler. However, because the NGen compilation must occur on the target processor architecture, this step is often performed when the user installs the application.

3.4 Common Type System (CTS) & Common Language Specification (CLS)

As mentioned previously, several different programming languages target the CLI, allowing, for example, code from C# sources to interact with code from Visual Basic. However, to achieve this feat, each language must have the same concept of how data types are stored in memory. The CTS, therefore, defines how a CLI-compatible language must view the bit patterns of values and the layout and behavior of objects to ensure interoperability.

The CLS is a subset of the CTS aimed at creating interoperable libraries.

3.5 The Framework (Base Class and Framework Class Libraries)

The CLI specifies a set of base classes that must be available to execute CLI code, otherwise known as the Base Class Library (BCL). The BCL contains Application Programming Interfaces (APIs) that enable executing CIL code to interact with the runtime environment and the underlying operating system.

Beyond the basics, there is also the .NET Framework Class Library (FCL). This Microsoft library contains APIs for creating graphical user interfaces, database applications, web access, and more.

3.6 Implementations of the CLI

Microsoft's implementation of the CLI stack is called .NET. Initially only available on Windows systems, Microsoft repackaged .NET in 2014 as an open-source, cross-platform development platform available on Windows, Linux, and macOS.

Another implementation Microsoft provides is Shared Source Common Language Infrastructure (SSCLI). SSCLI, however, is primarily a learning tool and, as such, is licensed under terms that prohibit use as the basis of commercial applications.

Finally, if you would like to develop apps for iOS and Android using C#, there is also the .NET MAUI implementation.

3.7 Take the knowledge test

Click the link below or scan the QR code to test your knowledge and understanding of C# Infrastructure:

https://www.answertopia.com/kbxm

3.8 Summary

The Common Language Infrastructure (CLI) provides a standardized environment for executing C# code. It includes the Common Intermediate Language (CIL), Virtual Execution System (VES), Common Type System (CTS), and Common Language Specification (CLS). The CLI enables interoperability between different programming languages and provides a base class library for executing CIL code.

In addition, the .NET Framework Class Library offers a vast collection of pre-built functions and classes for creating diverse applications and includes APIs for file I/O, networking, database access, and user interface design.

Chapter 4

4. Installing Visual Studio Code, C# and .NET 9

To begin programming in C#, we will need an environment to write, edit, compile, and run our code. There are many options, but for this book, we need a solution that is free to use and available to all readers, regardless of whether they are learning C# on macOS, Windows, or Linux systems. A popular tool, and the one we will be installing in this chapter, is Visual Studio Code. Developed by Microsoft, Visual Studio Code is a feature-rich, intuitive code editing environment, which, when combined with the C# Dev Kit extension, provides everything we need to learn C#.

4.1 Installing the .NET 9 SDK

In addition to installing Visual Studio Code, we will also need to install the .NET 9 SDK prior to compiling C# programs. While there are several ways to install .NET, we will use a technique that involves downloading and install the SDK independently from Visual Studio Code.

The .NET 9 SDK installation steps are specific to the operating system you are using as outlined below.

4.1.1 Installing .NET 9 on Windows

The .NET 9 SDK is available for Windows systems running on x86, x64, and Arm64 processor architectures. Using the following link, download the latest .NET 9 Installer package that matches your system:

https://dotnet.microsoft.com/en-us/download/dotnet/9.0

Once you have downloaded the installer, launch it and follow the setup wizard to complete the installation:

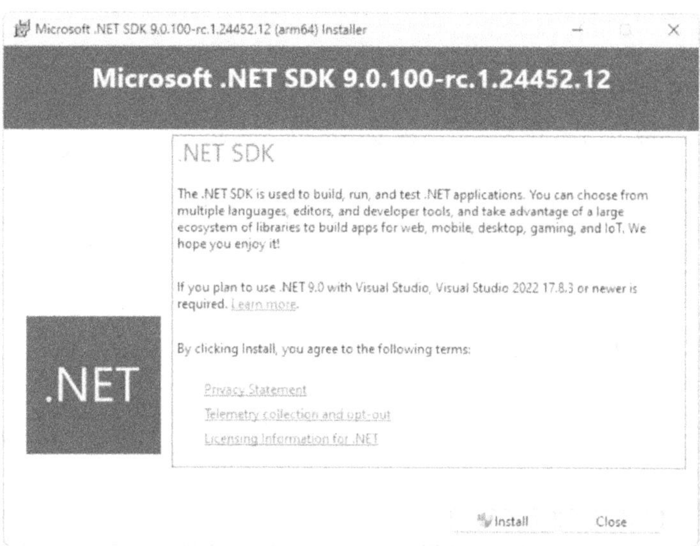

Figure 4-1

4.1.2 Installing .NET 9 on macOS

The macOS edition of the .NET 9 SDK is available or Intel and Apple Silicon systems. To begin the installation, open a browser window, navigate to the following URL, and download the Installer that matches your processor architecture:

https://dotnet.microsoft.com/en-us/download/dotnet/9.0

After downloading the Installer package, launch it and follow the steps to complete the installation:

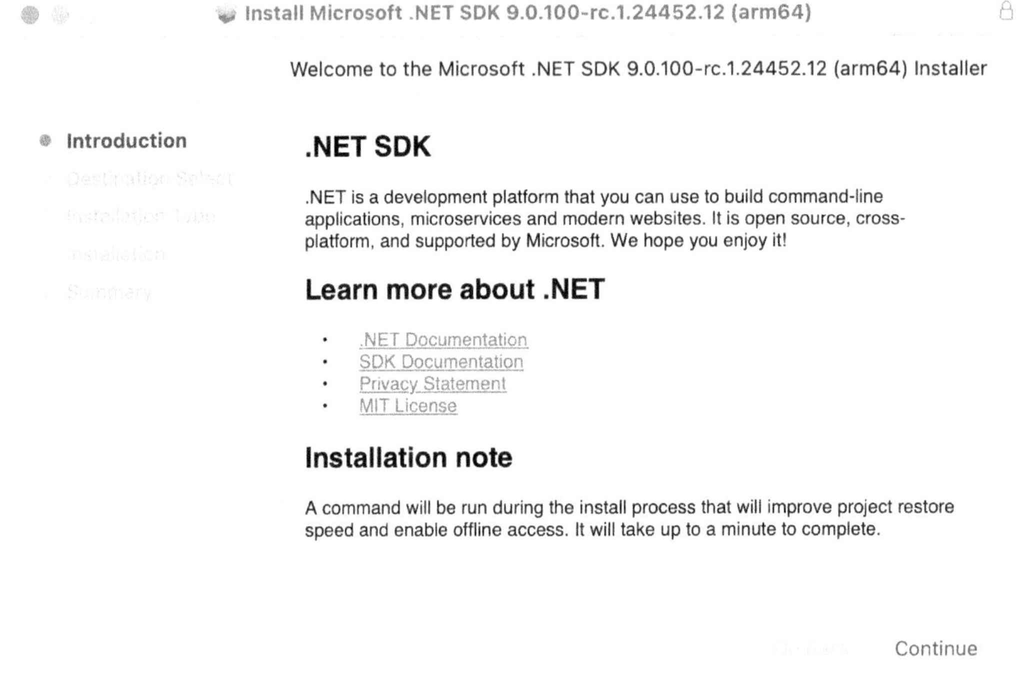

Figure 4-2

4.1.3 Installing .NET 9 on Red Hat Linux-based distributions

The best way to install the .NET 9 SDK on Linux distributions derived from Red Hat Enterprise Linux will depend on when you are reading this. At the time of writing, .Net 9 was still at the release candidate stage. It is possible that by the time you read this, .NET 9 will have been officially released. To find out, open a Terminal window and run the following command:

```
$ sudo dnf install dotnet-sdk-9.0
```

If the installation request reports that there is no match for dotnet-sdk-9.0, skip to the *"Installing .Net 9 from the Linux binaries"* section below to perform the installation. Otherwise, press 'y' to complete the installation.

4.1.4 Installing the .NET 9 on Debian/Ubuntu distributions

The installation steps for Debian and Ubuntu systems will, once again, depend on the release status of the .NET 9 SDK. Begin by running the following common in a Terminal window:

```
$ sudo apt-get install dotnet-sdk-9.0
```

If the installation request reports that the dotnet-sdk-9.0 package could not be found, skip to the next section to perform the installation. Otherwise, press 'y' to complete the installation.

4.1.5 Installing .Net 9 from the Linux binaries

If .NET 9 has not yet been officially released, the installation will need to be performed using the release candidate SDK binaries. Return to the .NET 9 download page and locate and download the binary that matches your CPU as highlighted in Figure 4-3:

OS	Installers	Binaries
Linux		Arm32 | Arm32 Alpine | Arm64 | Arm64 Alpine | x64 | x64 Alpine
macOS	Arm64 | x64	Arm64 | x64
Windows	x64 | x86 | Arm64 | winget instructions	x64 | x86 | Arm64
All	dotnet-install scripts	

Figure 4-3

Within a Terminal window, create a directory into which you would like to install .NET 9. Next, run the following commands (which assume you chose $HOME/dotnet9 as your installation directory):

```
$ cd $HOME/dotnet9
$ tar xvfz <path to downloaded binary archive>
```

After unpacking the .NET package, modify your *$HOME/.bashrc* file to export the DOTNET_ROOT environment variable and to add the .NET 9 SDK to your path:

```
export DOTNET_ROOT=$HOME/dotnet9
export PATH=$PATH:$HOME/dotnet9
```

Open a new Terminal window and run the following command to verify the installation:

```
$ dotnet --version
9.0.100-rc.1.24452.12
```

4.2 Downloading Visual Studio Code

The first step in installing Visual Studio Code (often abbreviated to VS Code) is downloading it. Downloads for Windows, macOS, and Linux are available from the following web page:

https://code.visualstudio.com/Download

4.3 Installing on Windows

Visual Studio Code for Windows is available for Arm and Intel-based systems. Once you have downloaded the installer, launch it and follow the setup wizard to complete the installation. You can use the default settings unless you have specific installation requirements.

4.4 Installing on macOS

Visual Studio Code is available for Apple Silicon and Intel-based systems and is provided as a ZIP archive file containing versions for both processor types. Once you have downloaded the file, double-click on it to extract the Visual Studio Code package, then open a second Finder window and drag the package to your Applications folder. For convenience, take this opportunity to drag Visual Studio Code to the Dock as shown in Figure 4-4 below:

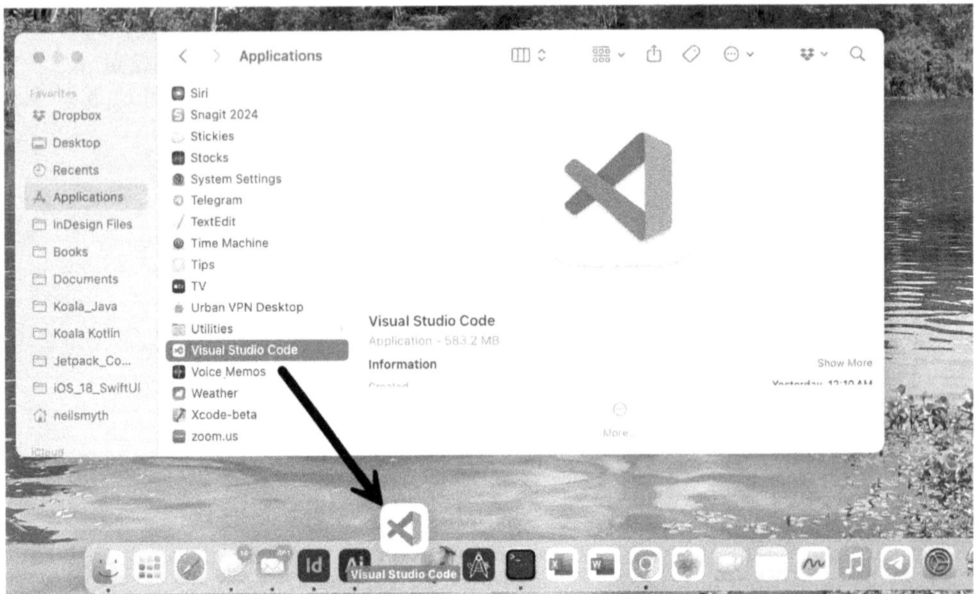

Figure 4-4

4.5 Installing on Linux

VS Code installation packages are available for several Linux distributions including Debian, Ubuntu, SUSE, and most Red Hat Linux-based platforms with support for x64, Arm32, and Arm64 processor architectures.

The steps to install VS Code will depend on which distribution you are running as outlined below:

4.5.1 Debian/Ubuntu

VS Code for Debian and Ubuntu is provided as a .deb package. To complete the installation, open a Terminal window, change directory to the location of the downloaded package, and run the following command (where *<filename>.deb* is the name of the package file):

```
$ sudo dpkg -i <filename>.deb
```

4.5.2 Red Hat-based distributions

VS Code is installed on Red Hat-based systems including RHEL, CentOS, Fedora, AlmaLinux, and Rocky Linux using a Red Hat Package Manager (.rpm) file. To install VS Code, open a terminal window, change directory to the location of the downloaded package, and run the following command (where *<filename>.rpm* is the name of the package file):

```
$ sudo rpm -ihv <filename>.rpm
```

After the installation completes, VS Code may be launched either by searching for the app in the desktop environment or via the command line by running the *code* executable.

4.6 Customizing Visual Studio Code

When VS Code runs for the first time, the screen shown in Figure 4-5 will appear. By default, the user interface will use the Dark Modern theme. If you prefer a different theme, make a selection from the option marked A below, or click the Browse Color Themes button (B) to browse the entire list:

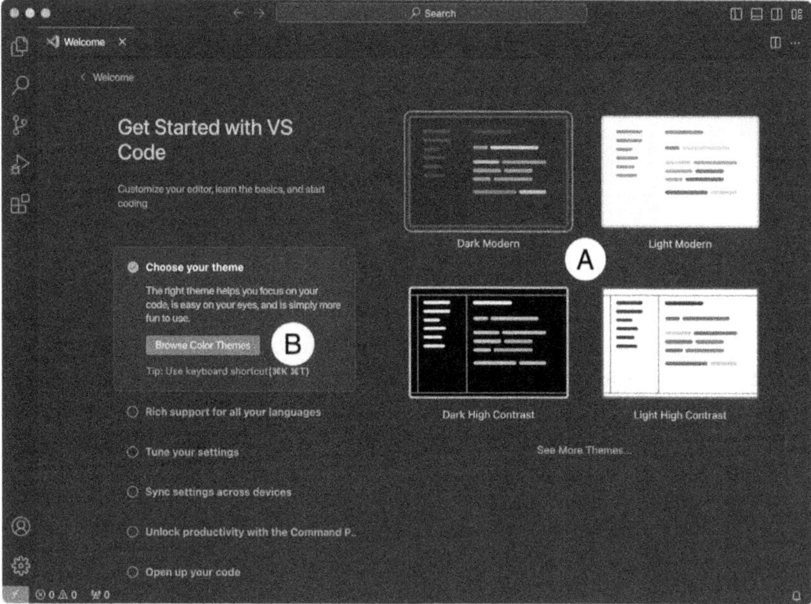

Figure 4-5

4.7 Adding the C# Dev Kit extension

The extension for C# development is the C# Dev Kit, and we will need to install it before we start writing code. To install the extension, click on the Extensions button located in the sidebar (marked A in Figure 4-6 below), then enter "C# Dev Kit" into the search field (B). Locate the C# Dev Kit entry in the extensions list and click the Install button (C) to add the extension:

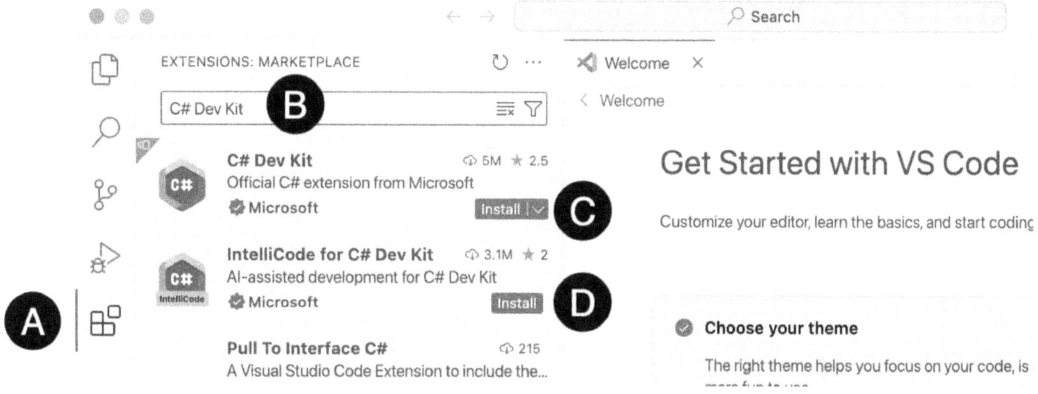

Figure 4-6

Another helpful extension when programming in C# is IntelliCode for C# Dev Kit. This extension uses AI to offer code completion suggestions as you type into the editor and is a valuable tool for increasing productivity and identifying ways to improve your code. Click the Install button marked D to add IntelliCode support to your VS Code configuration.

With the above steps completed, Visual Studio Code is installed and configured, and you are ready to start programming in C#.

4.8 Take the knowledge test

Click the link below or scan the QR code to test your knowledge and understanding of Visual Studio Code installation:

https://www.answertopia.com/iyjz

4.9 Summary

Visual Studio Code is a free code editing environment available for Windows, macOS, and Linux that, when combined with the C# Dev Kit extension, provides everything you need to learn C#. To install Visual Studio Code, download it from the official website and follow the installation instructions for your operating system. After installing Visual Studio Code, install the .NET SDK and the C# Dev Kit extension to enable C# development.

Chapter 5

5. A Guided Tour of Visual Studio Code

Now that we have installed VS Code, we must learn how to use it before we start writing C# code. In this chapter, we will take a guided tour of VS Code and cover the basics of using its key features. While an in-depth overview of every aspect of VS Code is beyond the scope of this chapter, the aim is to provide the skills needed to begin editing C# code with confidence.

5.1 Workspaces, projects, and solutions

When you start using VS Code, the first thing you will do is create a workspace. A workspace is a folder that contains one or more other folders. When you open a workspace, you will also open its subfolders. The terms workspace and folder are used interchangeably in the documentation and the menus within VS Code. For example, when you select the "Open Folder" option in VS Code, you are opening a workspace.

When working with C# and .NET in VS Code, each workspace subfolder generally contains a project. Each project represents a separate app, library, or service you are developing and contains all the source code and configuration settings to build it.

When you create your first C# project in VS Code, you will be asked to create or select a folder to contain the new project. The folder you choose will be the workspace in which the project resides.

In addition to the new project and workspace, VS Code will also create a solution file. The solution file references all of the projects within the workspace. Within VS Code, you will use the Solution Explorer to manage the projects in your workspace and perform tasks such as adding new classes or folders to an existing project.

5.2 The VS Code main window

Once you have created your first project, you will need to familiarize yourself with various elements that make up the VS Code user interface. Figure 5-1 shows a VS Code session with an open workspace containing multiple projects. The key areas of the main window are as follows:

A - **Activity Bar** - The activity bar contains buttons to display the primary sidebar, search project files, connect to Git source code repositories, run and debug code, browse and install extensions, and run tests. Options are also available to log into your Microsoft account and access settings.

B - **Primary Sidebar** - The primary sidebar is divided into three sections. The top section is the Explorer view, which lists all folders and files within the current workspace. Selecting a file from the list loads it into the editor (F).

C - **Outline** - The outline section of the primary sidebar displays the hierarchical structure of the currently selected source file, including symbols, classes, methods, and properties.

D - **Timeline** - The primary sidebar timeline panel lists recently performed activities such as saving, creating, or deleting project files.

E - Solution Explorer - This panel lists the files and folders referenced in the current solution file and allows tasks such as creating new classes to be performed.

F - Editor - The editor is where you will write and edit C# code. VS Code supports side-by-side and split editing modes where multiple files are open and visible simultaneously. Floating editor windows can also be detached from the main window.

G—Panel—The Panel includes tabs to display debug messages, problem reports, such as syntax errors in your code, and a terminal for interacting with your running apps.

H - Status Bar -The status bar includes fields indicating the editor's cursor line and column position, the current programming language, alert notifications, and error and warning statistics.

I - Run Button - Compiles and runs the current project app, displaying output in the Panel (G).

J - File Tabs - When multiple files are open, each file is represented by a tab in the File Tabs bar.

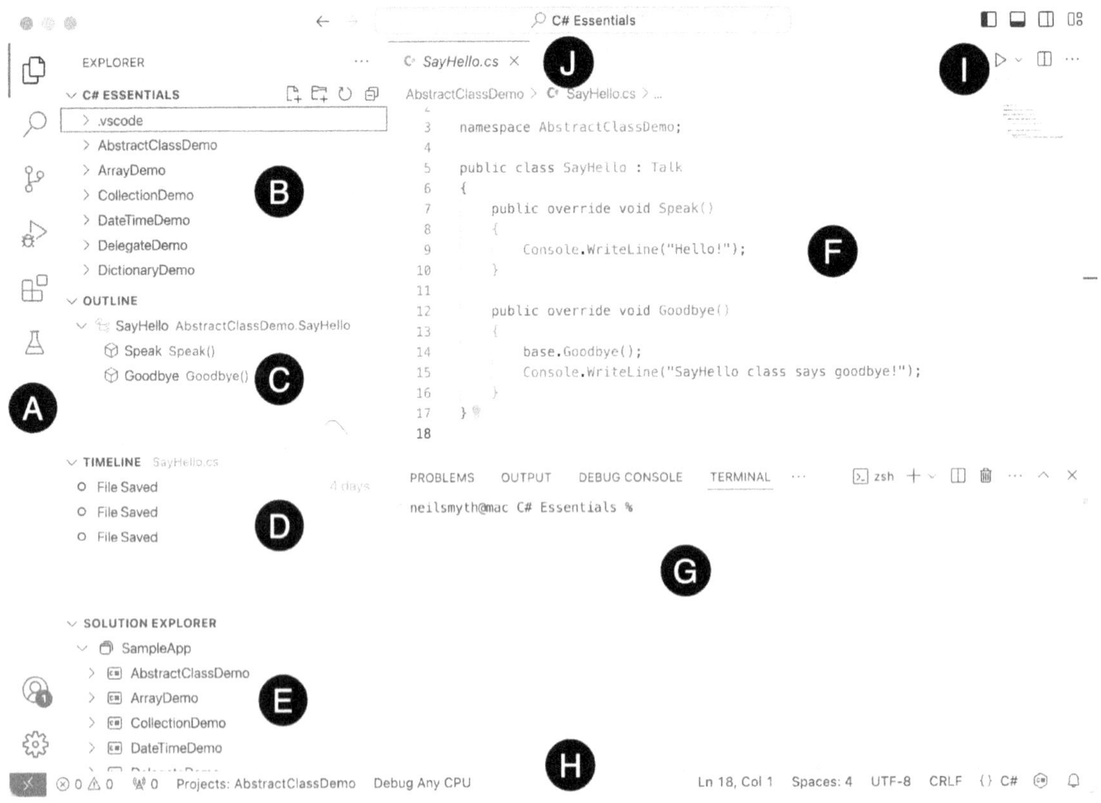

Figure 5-1

5.3 The Command Palette

The Command Palette is the central point for performing tasks within VS Code, including tasks as diverse as creating and cleaning projects, configuring keyboard shortcuts, and generating reports. Figure 5-2 shows a typical Command Palette:

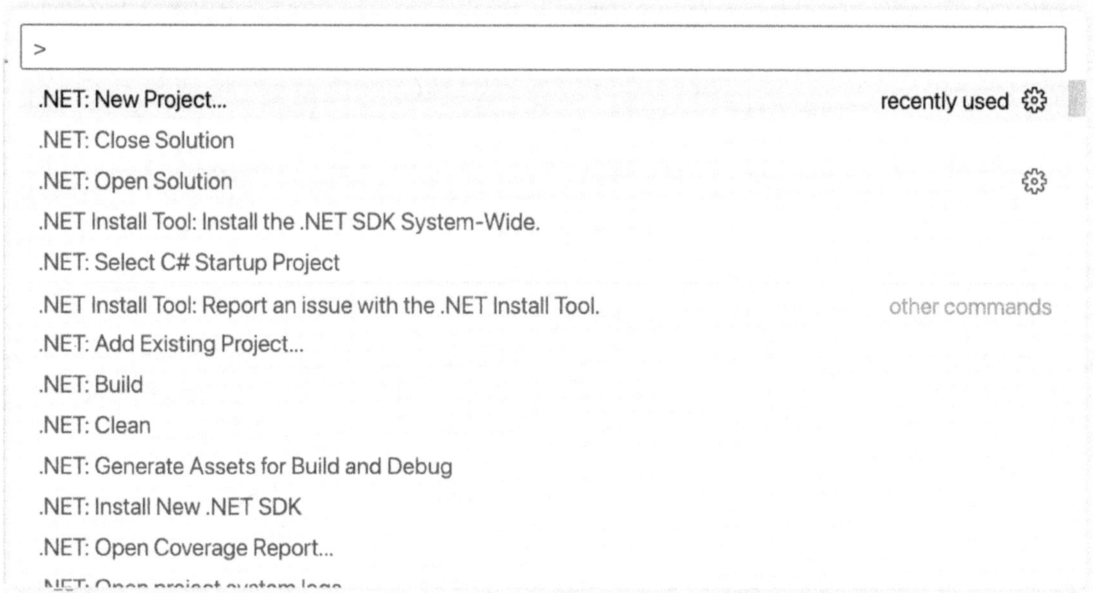

Figure 5-2

Display the Command Palette from anywhere in VS Code by pressing Ctrl-Shift-P (Cmd-Shift-P on macOS).

5.4 Splitting the editor window

When editing multiple files, it often helps to see the files side-by-side as you work. To split a file into a separate editor panel, right-click on the corresponding tab in the Files Tab bar and select the up, down, left, or right Split option as illustrated below:

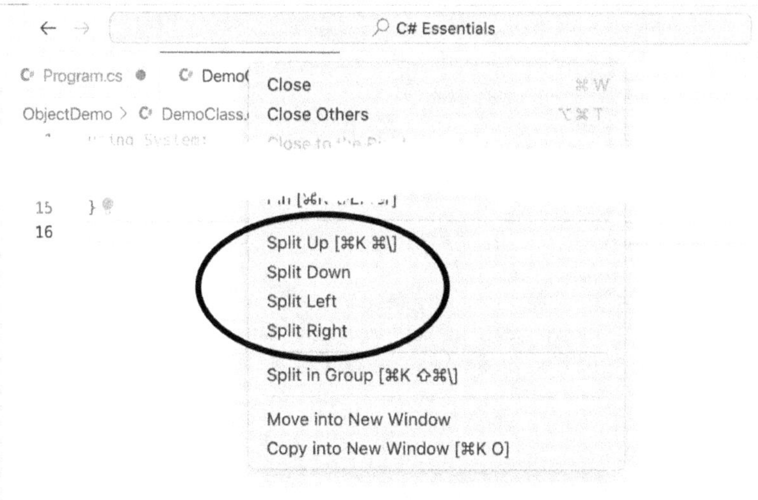

Figure 5-3

To open a file in a floating editor window, repeat the above step and select the Move into New Window menu option.

When editing large source files, it can be helpful to view and edit different areas of the same file simultaneously. To do this, right-click on the file tab and select the Split in Group menu option. A new editor panel containing the same code file will appear, and you can scroll to different file sections. Any edits that you make will be reflected in both editor panels.

5.5 Zen mode

The VS Code user interface can sometimes appear cluttered, particularly when the primary panel and console are displayed. To help you focus on writing code, VS Code offers Zen mode. In Zen mode, VS Code fills the entire screen, and only the current editing panels are visible. To enter Zen mode, select the *View -> Appearance -> Zen Mode* menu option or type Ctrl-K followed by Z (Cmd-K Z in macOS). Exit Zen mode by tapping the Esc key.

5.6 Learning with the Editor Playground

The VS Code Editor Playground (Figure 5-4) provides an interactive environment in which to learn and experiment with the features of the code editor. Select the VS Code *Help -> Editor Playground* menu option to display the playground, then follow the provided steps to interact with features including multi-cursor editing, formatting, and IntelliSense.

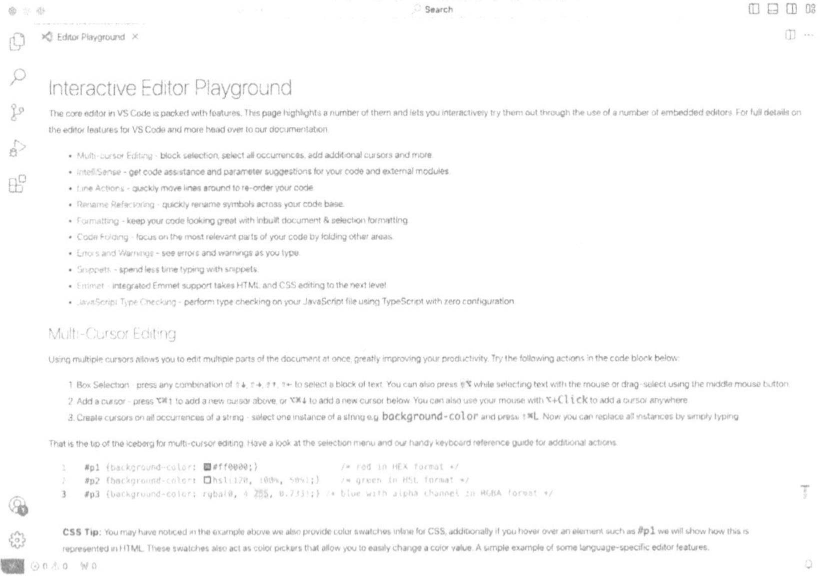

Figure 5-4

5.7 Take the knowledge test

Click the link below or scan the QR code to test your knowledge and understanding of the basics of Visual Studio Code:

https://www.answertopia.com/ix12

5.8 Summary

In this chapter, we have learned that VS Code organizes projects into workspaces, each containing one or more projects. The user interface includes the activity bar, primary sidebar, solution explorer, editor, and status bar. Most tasks outside general code editing are performed through the Command Palette. Zen mode hides distracting elements for focused coding, and the editor can be split to view and edit multiple files or different areas of the same file simultaneously.

Chapter 6

6. Creating an Example C# App in VS Code

The preceding chapters of this book have explained how to configure a C# development environment using Visual Studio Code and explored the tool's main features. Before moving on to slightly more advanced topics, now is a good time to validate that everything is installed and functioning correctly. The best way to achieve this is to create a C# app and compile and run it. This chapter will cover creating a C# console application project using VS Code.

6.1 Creating the SampleApp project

To begin, launch VS Code and display the Command Palette (Ctrl-Shift-P or Cmd-Shift-P). When the palette appears, locate and select the *.NET: New Project...* option.

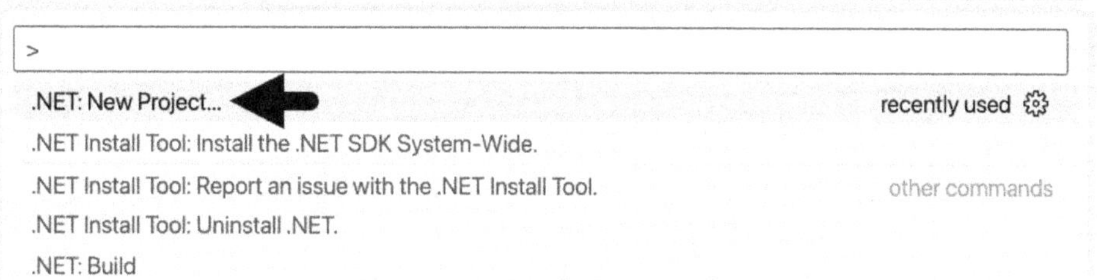

Figure 6-1

At this point, VS Code will ask us to select a project type. All the projects in this book will be console-based apps, so select the Console App project template option highlighted in Figure 6-2:

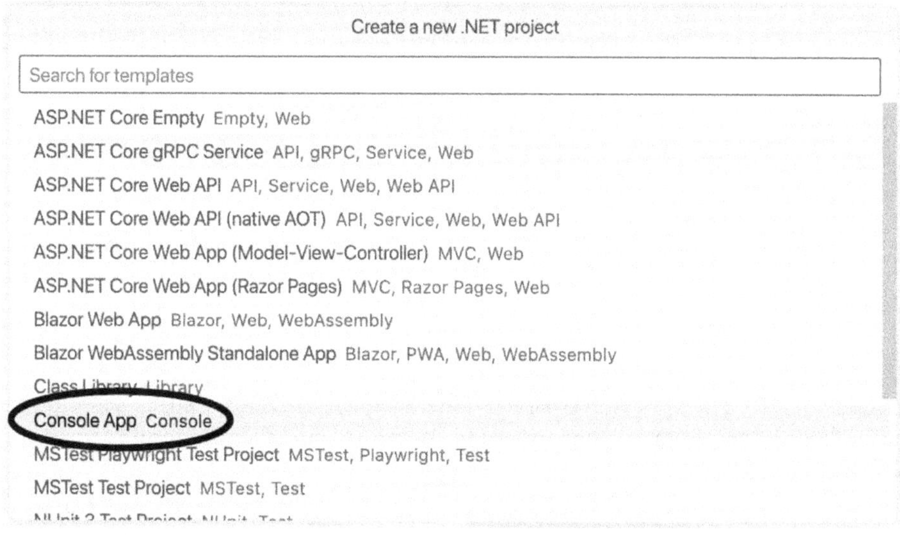

Figure 6-2

Once the project template has been selected, VS Code will display a file browser dialog. You will recall from the previous chapter that VS Code projects are stored in workspace folders. Since this is the first project we will create in VS Code, we will also need a workspace to contain it and the projects created in later chapters. Within the file browser, navigate to a suitable location on your file system and create a new folder named "C# Essentials" to serve as the workspace. Open the new folder to return to the Command Palette, name the project SampleApp, and press the Enter key:

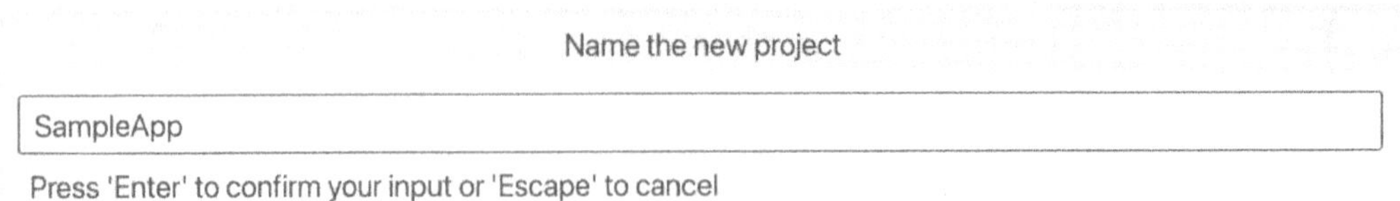

Figure 6-3

Finally, the Command Palette will seek confirmation that you wish to create the project in the designated workspace folder:

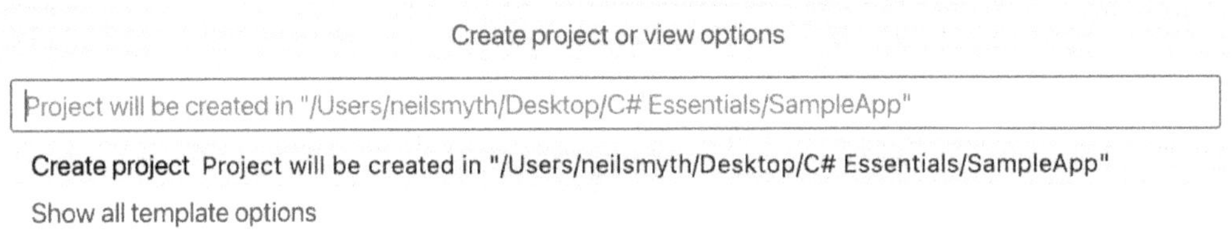

Figure 6-4

Review the workspace path, then press Enter to create the project.

6.2 Reviewing the SampleApp project

Now that we have created our first C# project, we can use the Explorer panel to review the files and folders that VS Code generated for us. If the Explorer is not already visible, select it using the action bar button indicated in Figure 6-5:

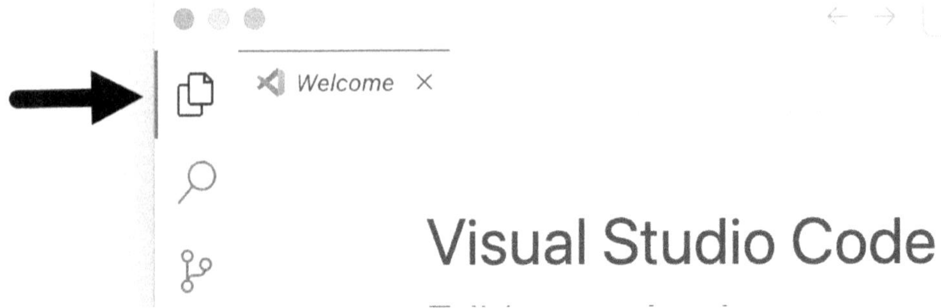

Figure 6-5

The Explorer lists our "C# Essentials" workspace and the SampleApp project folder. The arrows to the left of the workspace and project folder names (highlighted in Figure 6-6) are called disclosure arrows and are used to show and hide the folder contents:

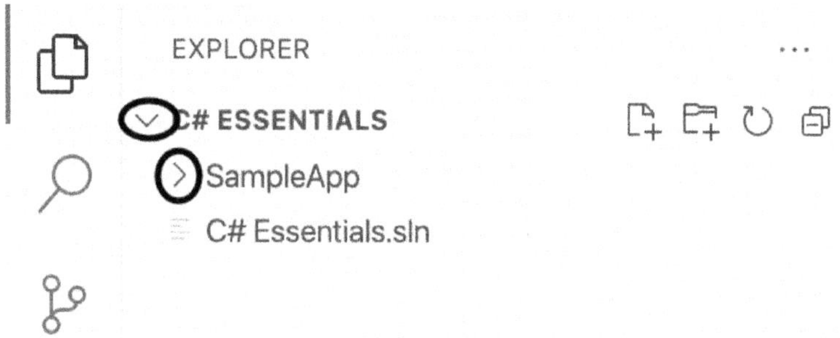

Figure 6-6

Click the disclosure arrow next to the SampleApp folder to view the files contained within the project:

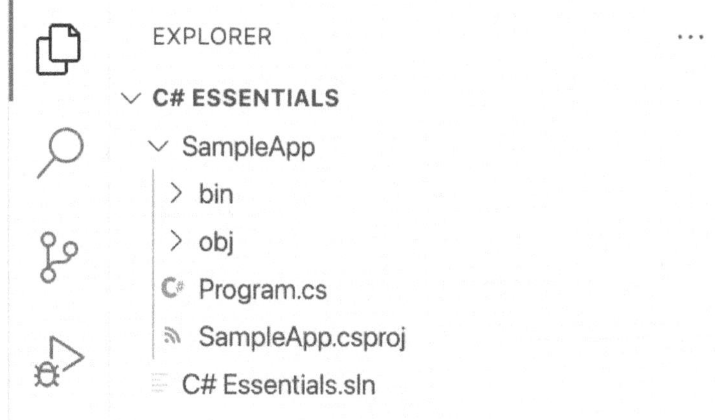

Figure 6-7

The two subfolders, named *bin* and *obj*, are used by VS Code when the app is compiled and run, and the *SampleApp.csproj* file stores the project's configuration settings. Select the *SampleApp.csproj* file to view its contents in the editor panel.

In addition to the workspace and project folder, VS Code has created a solution file named *C# Essentials.sln*, which contains references to the workspace projects. While selecting the solution file will display the content in the editor panel, a better option is to use the Solution Explorer as shown below:

Figure 6-8

VS Code also generated a file named *Program.cs*, where we will begin writing code.

6.3 Writing the app code

The *Program.cs* file represents the entry point into the app code when it runs. In other words, when we compile and run the app, the first lines of code to be executed will be those contained in the *Program.cs* file. Select the file to load it into the editor, where it will read as follows:

```
// See https://aka.ms/new-console-template for more information
Console.WriteLine("Hello, World!");
```

The first line is a comment informing us that the file uses the new console template. This template is particularly significant, as we will see later in the chapter. For now, we are more interested in the second line:

```
Console.WriteLine("Hello, World!");
```

The above line of code uses the WriteLine() method of the built-in Console class to display a message in the terminal window. To try out this code, click the run button shown in Figure 6-9:

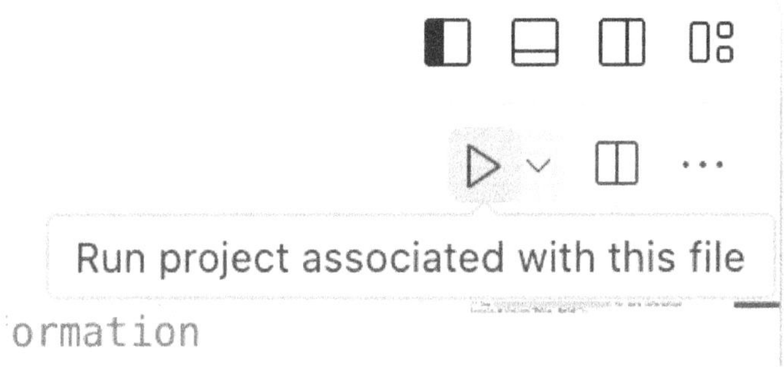

Figure 6-9

When the build process begins, refer to the Terminal in the bottom panel where, in addition to the diagnostic output, the "Hello, World!" output will appear:

```
PROBLEMS    OUTPUT    DEBUG CONSOLE    TERMINAL    PORTS

neilsmyth@mac C# Essentials % /Users/neilsmyth/.vscode/extensio
ns/ms-dotnettools.csharp-2.39.29-darwin-arm64/.debugger/arm64/vs
dbg --interpreter=vscode --connection=/var/folders/0b/m__39dws39
j_76pbx051h4nm0000gn/T/CoreFxPipe_vsdbg-ui-1120e8de0bb8410085877
97fd7c86ae0
Hello, World!
neilsmyth@mac C# Essentials %
```

Figure 6-10

The Terminal panel is a fully interactive environment. You can run commands just as you would in a Command Prompt on Windows or a terminal window on macOS or Linux.

Edit the *Program.cs* file and add the following lines:

```
Console.Write("Please enter your name: ");
var username = Console.ReadLine();
Console.WriteLine($"Hi {username}. Welcome to C#!");
```

The call to the ReadLine() method waits for keyboard input and assigns typed text to a variable called *username*:

```
Hello, World!
Please enter your name: John Smith
Hi John Smith, Welcome to C#!
```

6.4 Top-level statements and the Main method

The above example may be puzzling to those familiar with other programming languages in that we could write lines and execute code without any surrounding code structure or "instructions" to the compiler. Languages such as C# usually require additional information, such as a class name and directives to import framework dependencies. For example, our *Program.cs* file makes calls to methods belonging to the Console class, which, in turn, belongs to the System namespace, but we did not need to import that namespace into our code for it to run.

Another common requirement is to specify which code is the starting point for execution. Many programming languages have a special main function or method containing those initial lines of code. So if other programming languages have these requirements, why doesn't C#?

The answer is that C# has these requirements, but VS Code automatically generates these so-called top-level statements for us in the background. This is what the new console template comment in the *Program.cs* file was referring to. Although we only have four lines of code in our app, the actual code that gets compiled will resemble the following:

```
using System;

namespace SampleApp
{
    internal class Program
    {
        static void Main(string[] args)
        {
            Console.Write("Please enter your name: ");
            var username = Console.ReadLine();

            Console.WriteLine($"Hi {username}. Welcome to C#!");
        }
    }
}
```

The *using* directive in the above code tells the compiler to import the System namespace because the code in the file depends on it. Next, the internal class is wrapped in a namespace declaration called SampleApp. C# code contains classes, variables, and methods, all of which are assigned names. Namespaces allow application code to be organized so that the names in one workspace do not conflict with the same names in other workspaces. Anything declared outside of a namespace is part of the *global namespace*.

Within the SampleApp namespace, a Program class is declared to contain the Main() method, which, in turn, contains the app code.

You can override the default new console template behavior simply by declaring the above code in your *Program.cs* file. The choice of which approach to use is one of personal preference, though situations may arise where manually declaring the top-level statements is necessary. Therefore, it is important to understand what is happening behind the scenes.

6.5 Take the knowledge test

Click the link below or scan the QR code to test your knowledge and understanding of C# in Visual Studio Code:

https://www.answertopia.com/zkxb

6.6 Summary

In this chapter, we created a new workspace containing a .NET Console app project and explored the files that make up a typical project before writing, compiling, and running C# code. The chapter also introduced the concept of namespaces and explained how top-level statements and the Main() method are automatically generated by VS Code.

Chapter 7

7. C# Variables and Constants

To gain proficiency in any programming language, you need to learn the basics. One of the most fundamental aspects of programming is using variables and constants. Even advanced programs such as high-end video games and enterprise commerce applications utilize variables in some form.

This chapter will cover everything a C# programmer needs to know about variables and constants.

7.1 What is a C# variable?

Variables are locations in computer memory that are reserved for storing the data used by an application. Each variable is given a name by the programmer and assigned a value. The name assigned to the variable may then be used in the C# code to access the value assigned to the variable. This access can involve either reading the variable's value or changing the value. It is, of course, the ability to change the value of variables that gives them the name variable.

7.2 Type annotations and implicit typing

C# is categorized as a *type-safe* programming language. This essentially means that once a variable's data type has been identified, that variable cannot subsequently be used to store data of any other type without inducing a compilation error. This contrasts with *loosely typed* programming languages, where a variable, once declared, can subsequently be used to store other data types.

There are two ways in which the type variable will be identified. One approach is to use a type annotation when the variable or constant is declared in the code. This is achieved by preceding the variable name with the type declaration. The following line of code, for example, declares a variable named *userCount* as being of type int (integer):

```
int userCount = 10;
```

When using type annotation, a value may be assigned to the variable after it has been declared:

```
int userCount;
userCount = 10;
```

As an alternative to type annotation in a declaration, the C# compiler can use implicit typing to identify the variable type. When relying on implicit typing, the compiler looks to see what type of value is assigned to the variable when it is initialized and uses that as the type. To instruct the compiler to use implicit typing, you must precede the variable name with the *var* keyword.

Consider, for example, the following variable declarations:

```
var signalStrength = 22;
var companyName = "My Company";
```

While compiling the above lines of code, C# will infer that the *signalStrength* variable is of type int and that *companyName* is of type string.

When a variable is declared using implicit typing, it must be assigned a value at the point of declaration. The following, for example, is not valid C# syntax:

```
var bookTitle;
bookTitle = "C# 13 Essentials - .NET 9 Edition";
```

A new value may be assigned to a variable at any point after it has been declared:

```
int interestRate = 5; //Declare the variable and initialize it to 5
interestRate = 10; // variable now equals 10
```

7.3 What is a C# constant?

A constant is similar to a variable, providing a named location in memory to store a data value. Constants differ in one significant way: once a value has been assigned to a constant, it cannot subsequently be changed.

Constants are particularly useful if a value is used repeatedly throughout the application code. Rather than using the value each time, it makes the code easier to read if the value is first assigned to a constant, which is then referenced in the code. For example, it might not be clear to someone reading your C# code why you used the value 5 in an expression. If, instead of the value 5, you use a constant named interestRate, the purpose of the value becomes much more apparent. Constants also have the advantage that if the programmer needs to change a widely used value, it only needs to be changed once in the constant declaration and not each time it is referenced.

Constants are declared using the *const* keyword and have a type, a name, and a value:

```
const int interestRate = 10;
```

Note that a constant must be initialized at the point that it is declared. For example, the following code will fail to compile because it declares a constant without assigning a value:

```
const int interestRate; // Invalid - a constant must be initialized at creation
```

Now that we have described C# variables and constants, we can examine the different types available to us as C# programmers beginning with numerical data types.

7.4 Integer types

A widely used data type is the integer. C# provides several integer types based on number size and whether the integers are signed (positive or negative) or unsigned (positive only). All the integer variable types have one thing in common: they may only be used to store whole numbers.

The following table lists the various C# integer types, details of the number of bytes of physical memory consumed by each type, and the acceptable value ranges.

Type	Size in bytes	Value range
byte	1 byte	0 to 255
sbyte	1 byte	-128 to 127
short	2 bytes	-32,768 to 32,767
ushort	2 bytes	0 to 65,535
int	4 bytes	-2,147,483,648 to 2,147,483,647
uint	4 bytes	0 to 4,294,967,295
long	8 bytes	-9,223,372,036,854,775,808 to 9,223,372,036,854,775,807
ulong	8 bytes	0 to 18,446,744,073,709,551,615

Table 7-1

The following code demonstrates some of these data types:

```
int myInt = 2010210;
byte myByte = 233;
sbyte mySbyte = 127;
```

All C# numerical data types contain bounds properties that can be accessed to identify that particular type's minimum and maximum supported values. The following code, for example, outputs to the console the minimum and maximum bounds for some of the integer types listed above:

```
Console.WriteLine("byte Min Value = " + byte.MinValue);
Console.WriteLine("byte Max Value = " + byte.MaxValue);

Console.WriteLine("short Min Value = " + short.MinValue);
Console.WriteLine("short Max Value = " + short.MaxValue);

Console.WriteLine("int Min Value = " + int.MinValue);
Console.WriteLine("int Max Value = " + int.MaxValue);

Console.WriteLine("uint Min Value = " + uint.MinValue);
Console.WriteLine("uint Max Value = " + uint.MaxValue);

Console.WriteLine("long Min Value = " + long.MinValue);
Console.WriteLine("long Max Value = " + long.MaxValue);
```

The above code will generate the following output:

```
byte Min Value = 0
byte Max Value = 255
short Min Value = -32768
short Max Value = 32767
int Min Value = -2147483648
int Max Value = 2147483647
uint Min Value = 0
uint Max Value = 4294967295
long Min Value = -9223372036854775808
long Max Value = 9223372036854775807
```

7.5 Floating-point Variables

Integers are fine for dealing with whole numbers but of little use when there are numbers after the decimal point. Such numbers may be stored in float or double variable types. The default type for such numbers is double. The following table shows the two types with comparisons of the number ranges supported and the number of significant digits in each case:

Type	Size in bytes	Value range	Digit accuracy
float	8 bytes	+/-1.5 * 10–45 to +/-3.4 * 1038	6 – 7 digits
double	16 bytes	+/-5.0 * 10–324 to +/-1.7 * 10308	15 – 16 digits

Table 7-2

Since floating-point values in C# are considered to be double by default, it is not possible to declare a float variable as follows:

```
float myFloat = 23234.23;
```

An attempt to compile the above code will result in a syntax error that reads in part:

```
Literal of type double cannot be implicitly converted to type 'float'; use an 'F'
suffix to create a literal of this type
```

First, we need to understand what *literal* means in this context. Any value that is explicitly entered into C# code, such as a number (10, 23234.34, -11, etc.) or a string ("Hello World", "Dog" etc.), is referred to as a literal.

In the above example, a literal value of 23234.23 is assigned to a float variable named *myFloat*. The problem is that because floating-point literals are considered to be of type double this assignment cannot be made because the types don't match. Instead, we must tell C# that our literal number is actually of type float. This is achieved by placing an 'F' suffix at the end of the number literal as follows:

```
float myFloat = 23234.23F;
```

The following code demonstrates float and double declarations:

```
float myFloat = 312.20F;
double myDouble = 1856675407371955269.95;
```

It is important to note that float and double variables cannot be used as counting variables (for example, in looping constructs).

7.6 Decimal type

The integer and floating-point families of C# variable types have some limitations. Integers can only handle whole numbers, resulting in the fractional part of a value being stripped off. Floats, on the other hand, have problems with rounding accuracy. The best of both worlds is sometimes needed, and the decimal variable type is provided to address this situation. The decimal type is a compromise between integer and float variable types in that it can store fractional parts of a value and provide exact values in computations.

As with floating-point numbers, literal values must be declared as being of type decimal using an 'M' suffix. The following code declares two decimal values, multiplies them, and displays the result:

```
decimal val1 = 11231.582M;
decimal val2 = 43342.12M;

decimal result = val1 * val2;
```

7.7 Boolean type

The C# Boolean variable type is declared using the *bool* keyword and allows for storing true and false values. Boolean variables are helpful in control flow constructs such as *if* and *while* statements.

Unlike some other programming languages, C# Boolean variables must be assigned either true or false and cannot be assigned 1 or 0:

```
bool loopFinished = false;

if (loopFinished) {
  Console.WriteLine("The loop is complete");
} else {
  Console.WriteLine("Still looping");
}
```

Most software needs a way to store human-readable data in the form of characters and words. This chapter explores the use of string and character data types. The topic of building strings from multiple variables using a concept known as string interpolation is also covered.

Most software needs a way to store human-readable data in the form of characters and words. This chapter explores the use of string and character data types. It also covers building strings from multiple variables using a concept known as *string interpolation*.

7.8 Character data type

When talking about characters, we are referring to individual letters and numbers. For example, the letter 'a' is a character, as is the visual representation of the number '1'. Such characters may be stored in a C# char type. A char can contain one character and one character only. It is important to be aware that a character is not limited to those in the English alphabet. Characters are stored internally in C# as grapheme clusters. A grapheme cluster combines two or more Unicode scalars to represent a single visible character.

In addition, characters can be counted in loops and mathematical expressions. To assign a character to a variable or constant, surround the character with single quotes:

```
char myVar = 'a';
const char myConst = 'b';
```

The following lines assign a variety of different characters to char type variables:

```
char myChar1 = 'f';
char myChar2 = ':';
char myChar3 = 'X';
```

Characters may also be referenced using Unicode code points. The following example assigns the Unicode value for a four-pointed star symbol to a variable using Unicode and prints it:

```
char myChar4 = '\u2726';

Console.WriteLine(myChar4);
```

7.9 Special characters

In addition to the standard set of characters outlined above, a range of special characters (also called *escape sequences*) is available for specifying items such as a new line, tab, or a specific Unicode value within a string. These special characters are identified by prefixing the character with a backslash (a concept referred to as *escaping*).

For example, the escape sequence for a new line special character is \n. The following code fragment uses this new line special character to add blank lines within a string:

```
Console.WriteLine("This is a line of text.\n\n\nAn this is another.");
```

The above code will generate the following output:

```
This is a line of text.


An this is another.
```

Any character preceded by a backslash is considered a special character and treated accordingly. This raises the question of what to do if you want a backslash character. We achieve this by escaping the backslash itself (\\):

```
Console.WriteLine("C# special characters are escaped using the \\ character.");
```

When the above code executes, it will generate the following output:

```
C# special characters are escaped using the \ character.
```

Commonly used special characters supported by C# are as follows:

Constant	Special value
\e	Escape character
\n	Newline
\r	Carriage return
\t	Horizontal tab
\\	Backslash
\”	Double quote (used when placing a double quote into a string declaration)
\’	Single quote (used when placing a single quote into a string declaration)
\unn	Single-byte Unicode scalar where nn is replaced by two hexadecimal digits representing the Unicode character.
\unnnn	Double-byte Unicode scalar where nnnn is replaced by four hexadecimal digits representing the Unicode character.
\nnnnnnnn	Four-byte Unicode scalar where nnnnnnnn is replaced by eight hexadecimal digits representing the Unicode character.

Table 7-3

7.10 String data type

Previously, we looked at storing individual characters in a char variable. While this works for storing a single letter, number, or Unicode scalar, it is of little use for storing entire words or sentences. For this purpose, the string variable type is supported by C#. Constants or variables of type string can store a string of any number of characters.

String literal values are surrounded by double quotes ("). For example:

```
string myString = "This is string is literal.";
```

7.11 Verbatim string literals

A regular string value will interpret special characters. The following code, for example, consists of a string containing multiple special characters:

```
string myString = "This is some text\n\n\tand this is some more.";
```

As shown above, the only way to make the text span multiple lines is to use the \n escape character when using a standard string literal. The following code, for example, will not compile:

```
string myString = "This is some text

    and this is some more.";
```

A string literal must be declared as a *verbatim string literal* type for it to be interpreted precisely as written.

Verbatim string literals ignore the special meaning of escape characters and can span multiple lines. To declare a string literal as verbatim, prefix the declaration with the '@' character. For example, this allows literals such as the following to be expressed:

```
string myString = @"Hi Team,

The file located at 'C:\Users\demo\newdata.txt'

uses the \t sequence to insert tabs into text.

                Best regards

                        John";

Console.WriteLine(myString);
```

The above string literal will appear as follows when the code runs:

```
Hi Team,

The file located at 'C:\Users\demo\newdata.txt'

uses the \t sequence to insert tabs into text.

                Best regards

                        John
```

7.12 String interpolation

Strings may also be constructed using combinations of strings, variables, constants, expressions, and function calls using string interpolation.

Interpolation involves embedding items into a string by prefixing the literal declaration with a '$' character and wrapping the item as follows where *{item}* is a constant or variable name, a function call, or even an expression such as a mathematical calculation:

```
int count = 10;
string message = $"The current count is {count}";
```

The following code, for example, creates a new string variable using string interpolation to embed content from a variety of sources before outputting it to the console:

```
string userName = "John";
int inboxCount = 25;
int maxCount = 100;

var message = $"{userName} has {inboxCount} messages. Message capacity remaining
is {maxCount - inboxCount}.";

Console.WriteLine(message);
```

Running the above example code will generate the following:

```
John has 25 messages. Message capacity remaining is 75.
```

If you need to wrap content in braces ({}) without it being interpreted as interpolated values, use double braces ({{}}) as follows:

```
string userName = "John";
var message = $"{userName} reported seeing error code 10 {{low battery}}.";

Console.WriteLine(message);
```

On execution of the above code, the following text will appear:

```
John reported seeing error code 10 {low battery}.
```

Interpolation may also be used within verbatim string literals by prefixing the string with either $@ or @$:

```
string userName = "John";
int inboxCount = 25;
int maxCount = 100;

var message = $@"{userName} has {inboxCount} messages.

        Message capacity remaining is {maxCount - inboxCount}.";

Console.WriteLine(message);
```

The above code will generate the following output:

```
John has 25 messages.

        Message capacity remaining is 75.
```

Note that Interpolated string literals can only be assigned to variables. An attempt to assign an interpolated string to a constant will result in a compiler error.

7.13 Type casting

C# code works with many types, both provided by the language and many you will create yourself. This chapter explains how types may be related to each other while exploring the concepts of implicit and explicit type casting and obtaining an object's type.

As previously outlined, C# is a strongly typed language, meaning that once a variable has been declared as a particular type, it cannot subsequently be changed to a different type. This also restricts the type of value that can be assigned to the variable. It is not, for example, possible to assign a string value to an int variable.

Under some circumstances, however, assigning a value of one type to a variable of another type is possible. This involves the use of *implicit* and *explicit casting.*

7.13.1 Implicit casting

In instances where it is safe to do so without data loss, C# will allow you to assign a value from one type of variable to another simply using the assignment operator. For example, since a long variable is quite capable of storing any value that can be stored in an int variable, an assignment such as the following is perfectly valid:

```
int myInteger = 20;
long myLong;

myLong = myInteger;
```

This technique is called implicit casting since the casting from int to long is implied by the value type rather than explicitly declared within the code.

There are, however, limits to implicit casting. It is impossible, for example, to assign a long to an int using implicit casting because a long can store significantly larger numbers than an int (an int is 4 bytes in length versus 8 bytes for a long). Attempting to squeeze a long into an int variable would inevitably result in lost data. For this reason, the C# compiler will flag such an attempt as an error, and the code will fail to compile, as demonstrated below:

```
long myLong = 1381292100921;
int myInteger;

myInteger = myLong;
```

When the compiler encounters the above code, it will declare the following syntax error:

```
Cannot implicitly convert type 'long' to 'int'. An explicit conversion exists
(are you missing a cast?)
```

As the error message indicates, it may be possible to perform this operation using an explicit cast.

7.13.2 Explicit casting

While the compiler may prevent an implicit cast, it is possible that you, as the programmer, know that even though a variable is a long type, it will never contain a value greater than an int variable can store. In this case, you might legitimately want to assign the value stored in a long variable to an int variable. This can be achieved by using an explicit cast to convert the long value to an int.

Explicit casts are performed by placing the variable type to which you wish to convert in parentheses (()) before the name of the variable you want to convert from. The following code, for example, casts a long value to an int during an assignment operation:

```
long myLong = 138129210;
int myInteger;

myInteger = (int) myLong;
```

Care should be taken when using explicit casts. If the value being cast is greater than the storage capacity of the destination variable, the value will change without warning. For example, consider the following modification of the above example:

```
long myLong = 138129210212;
int myInteger;

myInteger = (int) myLong;

Console.WriteLine($"myLong = {myLong}");
Console.WriteLine($"myInteger = {myInteger}");
```

The output from the above code illustrates that the value assigned to *myInt* no longer matches that assigned initially to *myLong*:

```
myLong = 138129210212
myInteger = 690256740
```

In this case, the *myLong* value exceeds the int data type's storage capacity, causing the variable's value to change without warning. A bug of this nature may be difficult to locate in a complex development project.

Similarly, assigning a floating-point value to a variable that only stores whole numbers will result in the loss of the fractional part of the original value.

Note that casting is only possible on numerical data types. It is not, therefore, possible to perform casts on string, bool, or char data types.

7.13.3 Identifying variable's type

Identifying a variable's type in C# is also possible by calling the variable's GetType() method. The following code, for example, outputs the types of the *myVar1* and *myVar2* variables:

```
string myVar1 = "Hello";
double myVar2 = 123123.12;

Console.WriteLine(myVar1.GetType());
Console.WriteLine(myVar2.GetType());
```

The above string literal will appear as follows when the code executes:

```
System.String
System.Double
```

7.14 Take the knowledge test

Click the link below or scan the QR code to test your knowledge and understanding of C# variables and constants:

https://www.answertopia.com/q9yn

7.15 Summary

This chapter has begun introducing C# by exploring data types and providing an overview of how to declare constants and variables. It has also introduced concepts such as type safety and inference, special characters, and string interpolation. Finally, the chapter explained the difference between implicit and explicit casting and how these are used to change a variable's type.

Chapter 8

8. C# Operators and Expressions

This chapter covers using operators to create expressions when programming in C#, including arithmetic and assignment operators. Other topics covered include operator precedence, logical operators, and the ternary operator.

In the previous chapter, we used variables and constants in C# and described the different variable and constant types. However, being able to create constants and variables is only part of the story. The next step is using these variables and constants in C# code. The primary method for working with the data stored in constants and variables is in the form of expressions. This chapter will examine C# expressions and operators in detail.

8.1 What is an expression?

The most fundamental expression consists of an operator, two operands, and an assignment. The following is an example of an expression:

```
int theResult = 1 + 2;
```

In the above example, the (+) operator adds two operands (1 and 2) together. The assignment operator (=) subsequently assigns the result of the addition to an integer variable named *theResult*. The operands could have easily been variables or constants (or a mixture of each) instead of the actual numerical values used in the example.

In the remainder of this chapter, we will examine the various operators available in C#.

8.2 The basic assignment operator

We have already looked at the most basic of assignment operators, the = operator. This assignment operator assigns the result of an expression to a variable. In essence, the = assignment operator takes two operands. The left-hand operand is the variable to which a value is to be assigned, and the right-hand operand is the value to be assigned. The right-hand operand is, more often than not, an expression that performs some arithmetic or logical evaluation. The following examples are all valid uses of the assignment operator:

```
int x;
int y = 15;
int z = 5;

x = 10;  // Assigns the value 10 to a variable named x
x = y + z; // Assigns the result of variable y added to variable z to variable x
x = y;   // Assigns the value of variable y to variable x
```

Assignment operators may also be chained to assign the same value to multiple variables. For example, the following code assigns the value 20 to the *x*, *y*, and *z* variables:

```
int x, y, z;

x = y = z = 20;
```

8.3 C# arithmetic operators

C# provides a range of operators to create mathematical expressions. These operators primarily fall into the category of binary operators in that they take two operands. The exception is the unary negative operator (-), which indicates that a value is negative rather than positive. This contrasts with the subtraction operator (-), which takes two operands (i.e., one value to be subtracted from another). For example:

```
int y = -10; // Unary - operator used to assign -10 to a variable named y
int z = 2;

int x = y - z; // Subtraction operator. Subtracts z from y
```

The following table lists the primary C# arithmetic operators:

Operator	Description
– (unary)	Negates the value of a variable or expression
*	Multiplication
/	Division
+	Addition
–	Subtraction
%	Modulo

Table 8-1

Note that multiple operators may be used in a single expression, for example:

```
int y = 10; // Unary - operator used to assign -10 to a variable named y
int z = 2;

int x = y * 10 + z - 5 / 4;
```

While the above code is perfectly valid, it is essential to be aware that C# does not evaluate the expression from left to right or right to left but instead in an order specified by the precedence of the various operators that conform to basic mathematical principles. Operator precedence is an important topic to understand since it impacts the result of a calculation and will be covered in detail in the next section.

8.4 C# operator precedence

C# uses the same operator order concept as in basic mathematics. For example, we probably all learned from our school days that the answer to the following calculation is 210, not 300:

```
int x;

x = 10 + 20 * 10;
Console.WriteLine(x);
```

When the code runs, the generated result will be 210. This is a direct result of operator precedence. C# knows the same rules we learned at school that tell it which order operators should be evaluated in an expression. For example, C# correctly considers the multiplication operator (*) to be of higher precedence than the addition (+) operator.

Fortunately, the precedence built into C# can be overridden by surrounding the lower priority section of an expression with parentheses (another common concept in basic mathematics). For example:

```
int x;

x = (10 + 20) * 10;
```

In the above example, the expression fragment enclosed in parentheses is evaluated before the higher precedence multiplication, resulting in a value of 300.

The following table outlines the C# operator precedence order from highest precedence to lowest:

<table>
<tr><th>Precedence</th><th>Operators</th></tr>
<tr><td>Highest</td><td>+, -, !, ~, ++x, –x, (T)x</td></tr>
<tr><td></td><td>* / %</td></tr>
<tr><td></td><td>+ –</td></tr>
<tr><td></td><td><< >></td></tr>
<tr><td></td><td>< > <= >= is as</td></tr>
<tr><td></td><td>== !=</td></tr>
<tr><td></td><td>&</td></tr>
<tr><td></td><td>^</td></tr>
<tr><td></td><td>|</td></tr>
<tr><td></td><td>&&</td></tr>
<tr><td></td><td>||</td></tr>
<tr><td></td><td>:?</td></tr>
<tr><td>Lowest</td><td>=, *=, /=, %=, +=, -=, <<=, >>=, &=, ^=, |=</td></tr>
</table>

Table 8-2

It should come as no surprise that the assignment operators have the lowest precedence since you would only want to assign the result of an expression once that expression has been thoroughly evaluated. Don't worry about memorizing the above table. Most programmers use parentheses to evaluate their expressions in the desired order.

8.5 Compound assignment operators

C# provides several operators to combine an assignment with a mathematical or logical operation. These are primarily used when performing an evaluation where the result is to be stored in one of the operands. For example, one might write an expression as follows:

```
x = x + y;
```

The above expression adds the value contained in variable *x* to the value contained in variable *y* and stores the result in variable *x*. This can be simplified using the addition compound assignment operator (+=):

```
int x = 10;
int y = 20;

x += y;
```

The above expression performs the same task as x = x + y but saves the programmer some typing. This is yet another feature that C# has inherited from the C programming language. Numerous compound assignment operators are available in C#. The most frequently used are outlined in the following table:

Operator	Description
x += y	Add x to y and place the result in x
x -= y	Subtract y from x and place the result in x
x *= y	Multiply x by y and place the result in x
x /= y	Divide x by y and place the result in x
x %= y	Perform Modulo on x and y and place the result in x
x &= y	Assign to x the result of logical AND operation on x and y
x |= y	Assign to x the result of logical OR operation on x and y
x ^= y	Assign to x the result of logical Exclusive OR on x and y

Table 8-3

8.6 Increment and decrement operators

Another helpful shortcut involves the C# increment and decrement operators. As with the compound assignment operators described in the previous section, consider the following C# code fragment:

```
x = x + 1; // Increase value of variable x by 1
x = x - 1; // Decrease value of variable y by 1
```

These expressions increment and decrement the value of *x* by 1. Instead of using this approach, it is quicker to use the ++ and -- operators. The following examples perform the same tasks as the examples above:

```
x++; // Increment x by 1
x--; // Decrement x by 1
```

These operators can be placed either before or after the variable name. If the operator is placed before the variable name, the increment or decrement is performed before any other operations are performed on the variable. For example, in the following code, *x* is incremented before it is assigned to *y*, leaving *y* with a value of 10:

```
int x = 9;
int y;

y = ++x;
```

In the following example, the value of *x* (9) is assigned to variable *y* before the decrement is performed. Consequently, after the expression is evaluated, the value of *y* will be 9, and the value of *x* will be 8:

```
int x = 9;
int y;

y = x--;
```

8.7 Comparison operators

In addition to mathematical and assignment operators, C# includes a set of logical operators that help perform comparisons. These operators all return a Boolean (bool) true or false result depending on the comparison result and are binary in that they work with two operands.

Comparison operators are most frequently used in constructing program control flow. For example, an *if* statement may be built based on whether one value matches another:

```
int x = 9;
```

```
int y = 9;

if (x == y)
      Console.WriteLine("x is equal to y");
```

Output:

```
x is equal to y
```

The result of a comparison may also be stored in a bool variable. For example, the following code will result in a true value being stored in the variable named *result*:

```
bool result;
int x = 10;
int y = 20;

result = x < y;
```

Clearly, 10 is less than 20, resulting in a true evaluation of the x < y expression. The following table lists the full set of C# comparison operators:

Operator	Description
x == y	Returns true if x is equal to y
x > y	Returns true if x is greater than y
x >= y	Returns true if x is greater than or equal to y
x < y	Returns true if x is less than y
x <= y	Returns true if x is less than or equal to y
x != y	Returns true if x is not equal to y

Table 8-4

8.8 Boolean logical operators

Another set of operators that return Boolean true and false values is the C# Boolean logical operators. These operators both return Boolean results and take Boolean values as operands. The key operators are NOT (!), AND (&&), OR (||), and XOR (^).

The NOT (!) operator inverts the current value of a Boolean variable or the result of an expression. For example, if a variable named *flag* is currently true, prefixing the variable with a ! character will invert the value to false:

```
bool flag = true; //variable is true
bool secondFlag;

secondFlag = !flag; // secondFlag set to false
```

The OR (||) operator returns true if one of its two operands evaluates to true. Otherwise, it returns false. For example, the following code evaluates to true because at least one of the expressions on either side of the OR operator is true:

```
if ((10 < 20) || (20 < 10))
      Console.WriteLine("Expression is true");
```

Output:

```
Expression is true
```

The AND (&&) operator returns true only if both operands evaluate to true. The following example will return false because only one of the two operand expressions evaluates to true:

```
int x = 10;
int y = 20;

if ((x < 20) && (y < 10))
      Console.WriteLine("Expression is true");
else
      Console.WriteLine("Expression is false");
```

Output:

```
Expression is false
```

The XOR (^) operator returns true if one (and only one) of the two operands evaluates to true. For example, the following example will return true since only one operator evaluates to be true:

```
int x = 10;
int y = 20;

if ((x < 20) ^ (y < 10))
      Console.WriteLine("Expression is true");
else
      Console.WriteLine("Expression is false");
```

Output:

```
Expression is true
```

If both operands were evaluated to be true or both were false the expression would return false.

8.9 Range and index operators

The C# range (..) and index from end (^) operators allow you to declare value ranges, which are invaluable when working with collections such as arrays. The chapter titled *"Accessing and Sorting C# Array Elements"* will cover both of these operators.

8.10 The ternary operator

The C# ternary operator provides a shortcut way of making decisions. The syntax of the ternary operator is as follows:

```
[condition] ? [true expression] : [false expression]
```

The way this works is that [condition] is replaced with an expression that will return either true or false. The expression that replaces the [true expression] is evaluated if the result is true. Conversely, the [false expression] is evaluated if the result is false. Let's see this in action:

```
int x = 10;
int y = 20;

Console.WriteLine( x > y ? x : y );
```

Output:

```
20
```

The true and false expressions above simply output the largest value. In practice, this can be any valid expression. The following modification, for example, specifies a string value to be displayed for each outcome:

```
int x = 10;
int y = 20;

Console.WriteLine(x > y ? "x is larger" : "y is larger");
```

Output:

```
y is larger
```

8.11 Null-coalescing operators

The null-coalescing operator (??) allows a default value to be used if an operand has a null value. The syntax for using this operator is as follows:

```
<operand> ?? <default operand>
```

If the left operand is not null, then the operand's value is returned; otherwise, the expression returns the default operand value.

The following example will output text that reads "Welcome back, Customer" because the *customerName* variable is set to null:

```
string customerName = null;
string recipient = customerName ?? "Customer";

Console.WriteLine($"Welcome back, {recipient}");
```

Output:

```
Welcome back, Customer
```

C# also includes the null-coalescing assignment operator (??=), the syntax for which is as follows:

```
<operand1> ??= <operand2>
```

In this case, the value of operand2 will be assigned to operand1 only if *operand1* is null. Otherwise, *operand1* will remain unchanged.

In the following example, the value initially assigned to *customerName* remains unchanged since it does not contain a null value:

```
string customerName = "David";
customerName ??= "Customer";

Console.WriteLine($"Welcome back, {customerName}");
```

Output:

```
Welcome back, David
```

8.12 Bitwise Operators

As previously discussed, computer processors work in binary. These are essentially streams of ones and zeros, each one referred to as a bit. Bits are formed into groups of 8 to form bytes. As such, it is not surprising that we, as programmers, will occasionally end up working at this level in our code. To facilitate this requirement, C# provides a range of *bit operators*.

Those familiar with bitwise operators in other languages such as C, C++, and Java will find nothing new in this area of the C# language syntax. For those unfamiliar with binary numbers, now may be a good time to seek out reference materials on the subject in order to understand how ones and zeros are formed into bytes to form numbers. Other authors have done a much better job of describing the subject than we can do within the scope of this book.

For the purposes of this exercise we will be working with the binary representation of two numbers (for the sake of brevity we will be using 8-bit values in the following examples). First, the decimal number 171 is represented in binary as:

```
10101011
```

Second, the number 3 is represented by the following binary sequence:

```
00000011
```

Now that we have two binary numbers with which to work, we can begin to look at the C# bitwise operators:

8.12.1 Bitwise NOT

The Bitwise NOT is represented by the tilde (~) character and has the effect of inverting all of the bits in a number. In other words, all the zeros become ones and all the ones become zeros. Taking our example 3 number, a Bitwise NOT operation has the following result:

```
00000011 NOT
========
11111100
```

The following C# code, therefore, results in a value of -4:

```
int y = 3;
int z = ~y;

Console.WriteLine($"Result is {z}");
```

8.12.2 Bitwise AND

The Bitwise AND is represented by a single ampersand (&). It makes a bit by bit comparison of two numbers. Any corresponding position in the binary sequence of each number where both bits are 1 results in a 1 appearing in the same position of the resulting number. If either bit position contains a 0 then a zero appears in the result. Taking our two example numbers, this would appear as follows:

```
10101011 AND
00000011
========
00000011
```

As we can see, the only locations where both numbers have 1s are the last two positions. If we perform this in C# code, therefore, we should find that the result is 3 (00000011):

```
int x = 171;
int y = 3;
int z = x & y;

Console.WriteLine($"Result is {z}");
```

8.12.3 Bitwise OR

The bitwise OR also performs a bit by bit comparison of two binary sequences. Unlike the AND operation, the OR places a 1 in the result if there is a 1 in the first or second operand. The operator is represented by a single vertical bar character (|). Using our example numbers, the result will be as follows:

```
10101011 OR
00000011
========
10101011
```

If we perform this operation in a C# example the result will be 171:

```
int x = 171;
int y = 3;
int z = x | y;

Console.WriteLine($"Result is {z}");
```

8.12.4 Bitwise XOR

The bitwise XOR (commonly referred to as *exclusive OR* and represented by the caret '^' character) performs a similar task to the OR operation except that a 1 is placed in the result if one or other corresponding bit positions in the two numbers is 1. If both positions are a 1 or a 0 then the corresponding bit in the result is set to a 0. For example:

```
10101011 XOR
00000011
========
10101000
```

The result in this case is 10101000 which converts to 168 in decimal. To verify this we can, once again, try some C# code:

```
int x = 171;
int y = 3;
int z = x ^ y;

Console.WriteLine($"Result is {z}");
```

8.12.5 Bitwise Left Shift

The bitwise left shift moves each bit in a binary number a specified number of positions to the left. Shifting an integer one position to the left has the effect of doubling the value.

As the bits are shifted to the left, zeros are placed in the vacated right most (low order) positions. Note also that once the left most (high order) bits are shifted beyond the size of the variable containing the value, those high order bits are discarded:

```
10101011 Left Shift one bit
========
101010110
```

In C# the bitwise left shift operator is represented by the '<<' sequence, followed by the number of bit positions to be shifted. For example, to shift left by 1 bit:

```
int x = 171;
int z = x << 1;

Console.WriteLine($"Result is {z}");
```

When compiled and executed, the above code will display a message stating that the result is 342 which, when converted to binary, equates to 101010110.

8.12.6 Bitwise Right Shift

A bitwise right shift is, as you might expect, the same as a left except that the shift takes place in the opposite direction. Shifting an integer one position to the right has the effect of halving the value.

Note that since we are shifting to the right there is no opportunity to retain the lower most bits regardless of the data type used to contain the result. As a result, the low order bits are discarded. Whether or not the vacated high order bit positions are replaced with zeros or ones depends on whether the *sign bit* used to indicate positive and negative numbers is set or not.

```
10101011 Right Shift one bit
========
01010101
```

The bitwise right shift is represented by the '>>' character sequence followed by the shift count:

```
int x = 171;
int z = x >> 1;

Console.WriteLine($"Result is {z}");
```

When executed, the above code will report the result of the shift as being 85, which equates to binary 01010101.

8.13 Compound Bitwise Operators

As with the arithmetic operators, each bitwise operator has a corresponding compound operator that allows the operation and assignment to be performed using a single operator:

Operator	Description
x &= y	Perform a bitwise AND of x and y and assign result to x
x |= y	Perform a bitwise OR of x and y and assign result to x
x ^= y	Perform a bitwise XOR of x and y and assign result to x
x <<= n	Shift x left by n places and assign result to x
x >>= n	Shift x right by n places and assign result to x

Table 8-5

8.14 Take the knowledge test

Click the link below or scan the QR code to test your knowledge and understanding of C# operators and expressions:

https://www.answertopia.com/qo99

8.15 Summary

In C# programming, operators and expressions manipulate and evaluate variables and constants. This can be as simple as adding two numbers using the addition operator in an expression and storing the result in a variable or as complex as performing bitwise operations. There are several categories of operators, each of which we have covered in this chapter.

Chapter 9

9. C# Conditional Control Flow

The cornerstone of any software code is the control flow logic, which decides which code should be executed and which should not. This chapter covers the conditional control flow constructs provided by C#.

9.1 Looping vs. conditional control flow

Regardless of the programming language used, application development involves applying logic. Much of the art of programming involves writing code that makes decisions based on one or more criteria. Such decisions define which code gets executed, how often, and which code gets bypassed when the program runs. This is often called control flow since it controls the program execution flow. Control flow typically falls into the categories of looping control flow (how often code is executed) and conditional control flow (whether code is executed). This chapter provides an introductory overview of both types of control flow in C#.

Earlier in the book, we used logical expressions in C# to determine whether something is true or false. Much of the art of programming involves writing code that makes decisions based on one or more criteria. Such decisions define which code gets executed and which gets bypassed when running the program.

In previous chapters, the *if* statement has been used in some examples. In this chapter, we will look at *if* statements in more detail.

9.2 Using the if statement

The *if* statement is the most basic of the control flow options available to the C# programmer. Programmers familiar with C, C++, or Java will immediately be comfortable using C# *if* statements.

The basic syntax of the C# *if* statement is as follows:

```
if (boolean expression) {
    // C# code to be performed when the expression evaluates to true here
}
```

If the boolean expression evaluates to true, then the code in the statement's body is executed. The body of the statement is enclosed in braces ({}). If, on the other hand, the expression is evaluated as false, the code in the body of the statement is skipped.

For example, if a decision needs to be made depending on whether one value is greater than another:

```
int x = 10;

if ( x > 9 ) {
      Console.WriteLine("x is greater than 9!");
}
```

Clearly, *x* is greater than 9, causing the message to appear.

Note: If the body contains only one statement, the enclosing braces ({}) may be omitted. These must be added once more than one statement is included in the body.

9.3 Using if … else … statements

The next variation of the *if* statement allows us to specify some code to execute if the expression in the *if* statement is evaluated as false using the following syntax:

```
if (boolean expression) {
    // Code to be executed if the expression is true
} else {
    // Code to be executed if the expression is false
}
```

Using the above syntax, we can now extend our previous example to display a different message if the comparison expression evaluates to be false:

```
int x = 8;

if ( x > 9 ) {
    Console.WriteLine("x is greater than 9!");
} else {
    Console.WriteLine("x is less than 9!");
}
```

In this case, the second WriteLine() statement would execute if the value of *x* was less than 9.

As with the standalone *if* statement, the braces ({}) are optional if the body only contains one statement. The following is, therefore, valid code:

```
int x = 8;

if ( x > 9 ) {
    Console.WriteLine("x is greater than 9!");
} else {
    Console.WriteLine("x is less than 9!");
}
```

9.4 Using if … else if … statements

So far, we have looked at *if* statements that make decisions based on the result of a single logical expression. Sometimes, it becomes necessary to make decisions based on several different criteria. For this purpose, we can use the *if … else if …* construct, the syntax for which is as follows:

```
if (boolean expression) {
    // Code to be executed if the expression is true
} else if (boolean expression) {
    // Code to be executed if the expression is true
} else if .....

} else {
    // Code to be executed if previous expressions are all false
}
```

Note: The final *else* can be omitted if no action is to be taken if all the boolean expressions evaluate to a false result.

The following code excerpt demonstrates the use of the *if ... else if ...* construct:

```
int x = 11;

if (x == 10) {
    Console.WriteLine("x is 10");
} else if (x == 9) {
    Console.WriteLine("x is 9");
} else if (x == 8) {
    Console.WriteLine("x is 8");
} else {
    Console.WriteLine("x is some other number");
}
```

This approach works well for a moderate number of comparisons but can become cumbersome for a larger volume of expression evaluations. The C# *switch* statement provides a more flexible and efficient solution for such situations. The *switch* statement will be covered in the next chapter.

9.5 Take the knowledge test

Click the link below or scan the QR code to test your knowledge and understanding of C# control flow:

https://www.answertopia.com/xzu2

9.6 Summary

The term control flow describes the logic that dictates the execution path through an application's source code as it runs. This chapter has examined conditional control flow and explored how the *if* and *else* statements are used to implement this type of flow logic.

Chapter 10

10. The C# switch Statement

In this chapter, we will introduce the C# *switch* statement and demonstrate why it is a better alternative to complicated *if... else if...* statements.

In the previous chapter, we looked at controlling program execution flow using the *if* and *else* statements. While these statement constructs work well for testing a limited number of conditions, they quickly become unwieldy when dealing with more significant numbers of possible conditions. C# has inherited the *switch* statement from the C programming language.

In this chapter, we will explore the *switch* statement in detail.

10.1 Why use the switch statement?

For a few logical value evaluations, the *if ... else if ...* construct is perfectly adequate. Unfortunately, any more than two or three possible scenarios can quickly make such a construct both time-consuming to write and difficult to read. As a case in point, consider the following code example. The program uses *if ... else if ...* statements to identify the manufacturer of a car based on the model name:

```
string carModel = "Corolla";
string carManufacturer;


if ((String.Compare(carModel, "Patriot") == 0) ||
    (String.Compare(carModel, "Liberty") == 0) ||
    (String.Compare(carModel, "Wrangler") == 0)) {
    carManufacturer = "Jeep";
}
else if (String.Compare(carModel, "Focus") == 0) {
    carManufacturer = "Ford";
}
else if (String.Compare(carModel, "Corolla") == 0) {
    carManufacturer = "Toyota";
} else {
    carManufacturer = "unknown";
}


Console.WriteLine($"Manufacturer is {carManufacturer}");
```

While the code is not excessive, it is already starting to become somewhat hard to read and takes more time to write than necessary. Imagine, however, if instead of 3 car models, we had to test for 10 or 20 models. Clearly, a more straightforward solution is needed, and that solution is the *switch* statement.

10.2 Using the switch statement

The syntax for a C# *switch* statement is as follows:

```
switch (value){
     case constant:
```

```
            statements
            break/jump

      case constant:
            statements
            break/jump

      default:
            statements
            break/jump
}
```

This syntax needs some explanation before we create a *switch*-based version of the above *if… else if…* construct.

In the above syntax outline, *value* represents either a value or an expression that returns a value. This is the value against which the *switch* operates. Using our example, this would be the string representing the car model.

A case statement is required for each possible match, followed by a constant value (once again, using our example, this would be the car models). Each case constant must be of the same type as the governing value. Following the case line are the C# statements to be executed if the value matches the case constant.

After the statements comes an optional *break*, *goto*, or *continue* statement. These statements break out of the *switch* statement when a match is found, jump to a specific location in the code, or skip any remaining code in a loop and begin the next iteration.

Finally, the *default:* section of the construct defines what should happen if none of the case statements present a match to the value.

10.3 A switch statement example

With the above information in mind, we may now construct a *switch* statement that provides the same functionality as our previous and somewhat unwieldy *if… else if…* construct:

```
string carModel = "Corolla";
string carManufacturer;

switch (carModel) {
    case "Patriot":
    case "Liberty":
    case "Wrangler":
        carManufacturer = "Jeep";
        break;
    case "Focus":
        carManufacturer = "Ford";
        break;
    case "Corolla":
        carManufacturer = "Toyota";
        break;
    default:
        carManufacturer = "unknown";
        break;
```

```
}

Console.WriteLine($"Manufacturer is {carManufacturer}");
```

10.4 Explaining the example

In the above example, the string assigned to the *carModel* variable is used as the governing variable in the *switch* statement. As with the Jeep manufacturer, case statements may be grouped, preceding a single set of statements.

The default option sets the *carManufacturer* string to “unknown” if none of the case statements match the car model string.

10.5 Using switch expressions

Using a *switch* statement has saved us some typing and made the code easier to read, but C# allows us to further simplify the code using *switch expressions*, the syntax for which is as follows:

```
result = value switch
{
    constant1 => statements,
    constant2 => statements,
    constant3 or constant4 or ... => statements,
    constant5 and constant 6 or constant7 => statements,
    _ => default_statement
};
```

Using a switch expression, our example can be simplified as follows:

```
string carModel = "Corolla";
string carManufacturer;

carManufacturer = carModel switch
{
    "Patriot" or "Liberty" or "Wrangler" => "Jeep",
    "Focus" => "Ford",
    "Corolla" => "Toyota",
    _ => "unknown"
};

Console.WriteLine($"Manufacturer is {carManufacturer}");
```

10.6 Using goto in a C# switch statement

In our original example, we used the *break* statement to exit out of the *switch* statement. The result of this is to move the point of program execution to the statements immediately following the *switch* statement. Unfortunately, this presents a problem when the default statements must be executed. To address this requirement, we can replace the *break* statements in our example code with a *goto* default statement:

```
string carModel = "Corolla";
string carManufacturer = "unknown";

switch (carModel) {
    case "Patriot":
    case "Liberty":
```

```
    case "Wrangler":
        carManufacturer = "Jeep";
        goto default;
    case "Focus":
        carManufacturer = "Ford";
        goto default;
    case "Corolla":
        carManufacturer = "Toyota";
        goto default;
    default:
        Console.WriteLine($"The {carModel} is manufactured by
{carManufacturer}");
        break;
}
```

While the *goto* statement could also be used to jump to a labeled location in our C# code, using it in this way is strongly discouraged. The above-mentioned use is the only acceptable use of the *goto* statement in a modern object-oriented language such as C#. As any veteran programmer will tell you, if you find yourself in a position where a *goto* statement is your only way of achieving something, you need to re-think and re-structure your code so that you no longer need the *goto*.

10.7 Using continue in a C# switch statement

Another alternative to the *break* statement is the *continue* statement. Suppose the *switch* statement is part of a loop. In that case, the *continue* statement will cause execution to return immediately to the beginning of the loop, bypassing any subsequent code yet to be executed in the current loop iteration.

The use of the *continue* statement in loops will be covered in the *"C# Looping with the for Statement"* chapter.

10.8 Take the knowledge test

Click the link below or scan the QR code to test your knowledge and understanding of the C# switch statement:

https://www.answertopia.com/k4uy

10.9 Summary

The *if-else* statement is a reliable way to make decisions when there are only a few possible outcomes. However, when many potential outcomes result from an evaluation, this approach can become cumbersome. In such cases, the *switch* statement is a better option for implementing flow control logic in C#. A *switch* statement may be further simplified in many situations using a *switch expression*.

Chapter 11

11. C# Looping with the for Statement

This chapter will continue looking at control flow in C# code. In the preceding chapters, we have examined using logical expressions to decide what C# code should be executed. Another aspect of control flow entails the definition of loops. Loops are sequences of C# statements that execute repeatedly until a specified conditions are met.

11.1 Why use loops?

It is generally common knowledge that computers are great at performing repetitive tasks an infinite number of times and doing so very quickly. It is also common knowledge that computers really don't do anything unless someone programs them to tell them what to do. Loop statements are the primary mechanism for telling a computer that a sequence of tasks needs to be repeated a specific number of times. Suppose, for example, that you need to add a number to itself ten times. One way to do this might be to write the following C# code:

```
long j = 1;


j += j;
j += j;
j += j;
j += j;
j += j;
j += j;
j += j;
j += j;
j += j;
j += j;
```

While somewhat cumbersome, this does work. What would happen if you needed to perform this task 100 or even 10,000 times? Writing C# code to perform this as above would be prohibitive. Such a scenario is precisely what the *for* loop is intended to handle.

The syntax of a C# *for* loop is as follows:

```
for ( <initializer>; <conditional expression'>; <loop expression> )
{
      statements to be executed
}
```

The *<initializer>* element initializes a counter variable. Traditionally, the variable *i* is used for this purpose. For example:

```
i = 0;
```

The code above sets the counter to be variable *i* and sets it to zero. Note that if the counter variable has not been previously declared, it may be declared as part of the *for* statement:

```
int i = 0;
```

The conditional expression specifies the test to verify whether the loop has performed the required number of iterations. For example, if we want to loop 100 times:

```
i < 100;
```

Finally, the loop expression specifies the action to perform on the counter variable. For example, to increment by 1:

```
i++;
```

The body of statements to be executed on each iteration of the loop is contained within the code block defined by the opening ({) and closing (}) braces.

By bringing this all together, we can create a *for* loop to perform the task outlined in the earlier example:

```
long j = 1;

for (int i=0; i<50; i++) {
        j += j;
        Console.WriteLine("j = " + j);
}
```

11.2 C# loop variable scope

A key point to note in creating loops is that any variables defined within the body of a loop are only visible to code within the loop. This is a concept known as scope. If, for example, a variable *myCounter* is defined within the body of a *for* loop, that variable ceases to exist once the loop terminates:

```
// variable myCounter does not yet exist

for (int i = 0; i < 10; i++)
{
        int myCounter = 0; //myCounter variable created in scope of for loop
        myCounter += i;
}

// after loop exit variable myCounter is now out of scope and ceases to exist
```

11.3 Creating an infinite for loop

A *for* loop, which will execute an infinite number of times, may be constructed using *for (;;)* syntax. For example, the following code sample will output “Hello from C#” until the program is manually terminated by the user (or the computer is turned off or rebooted):

```
for (;;)
{
    Console.WriteLine("Hello from C#");
}
```

If you try the above example in VS Code and find yourself in an infinite loop, you can stop execution using the stop button highlighted in Figure 11-1 below:

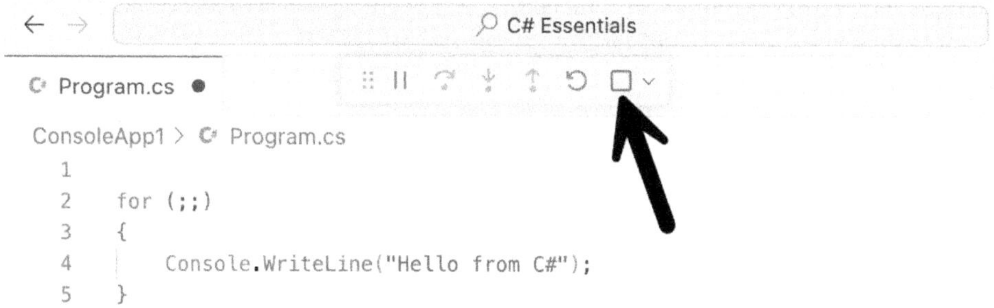

Figure 11-1

11.4 Breaking out of a for loop

Having created a loop, you might want to break out of it under certain conditions before the completion criteria have been met (particularly if you have created an infinite loop). One such example might involve continually checking for activity on a network socket. Once the activity has been detected, it will be necessary to break out of the monitoring loop and perform some other task.

To break out of a loop, C# provides the *break* statement, which breaks out of the current loop and resumes execution at the code directly after the loop. For example:

```
int j = 10;

for (int i = 0; i < 50; i++)
{
      j += j;

      Console.WriteLine("j = " + j);

      if (j > 100)
            break;
}
```

In the above example, the loop will continue to execute until the value of *j* exceeds 100, at which point the loop will exit.

11.5 Nested for loops

So far, we have looked at only a single level of *for* loop. It is also possible to nest *for* loops where loops reside inside other loops. For example:

```
for (int i = 0; i < 100; i++) {
      Console.WriteLine( "i = " + i);

      for (int j = 0; j < 10; j++) {
                Console.WriteLine( "j = " + j);
      }
}
```

The above example will loop 100 times, displaying the value of *i* on each iteration. In addition, each of those iterations will loop 10 times, displaying the value of *j*.

The above example shows two levels of nesting. Of course, it is possible to nest to more levels, though too many levels may result in difficult-to-understand code.

11.6 Breaking from nested loops

An important point to be aware of when breaking out of a nested *for* loop is that the break only exits from the current level of the loop. For example, the following C# code example will exit from the current iteration of the nested loop when *j* equals 5. The outer loop will, however, continue to iterate and, in turn, execute the nested loop:

```
for (int i = 0; i < 100; i++) {
      Console.WriteLine( "i = " + i);


      for (int j = 0; j < 10; j++) {
          if (j == 5)
               break;
               Console.WriteLine( "j = " + j);
      }
}
```

11.7 Continuing for loops

Another helpful statement for use in loops is the *continue* statement. When the execution process finds a *continue* statement in any loop, it skips all remaining code in the loop's body and begins execution again from the top of the loop. Using this technique, we can, for example, construct a *for* loop that outputs only even numbers between 1 and 9:

```
for (int i = 1; i < 10; i++) {
      if ((i % 2) != 0)
            continue;
      Console.WriteLine($"i = {i}");
}
```

In the example, if *i* is not divisible by 2 with 0 remaining, the code performs a *continue* operation, sending execution to the top of the *for* loop, thereby bypassing the code to output the value of *i*. This results in only even numbers appearing in the console.

11.8 The C# foreach statement

The *foreach* loop is used to iterate over a sequence of items in a collection and provides a simple-to-use looping option.

The syntax of the *foreach* loop is as follows:

```
foreach <name> in <collection> {
     // code to be executed
}
```

In this syntax, <name> is the name for a constant containing the current item from the object through which the loop is iterating. The code in the loop's body will typically use this constant name to reference the current item in the loop cycle. The <collection> is the object through which the loop is iterating. This could, for example, be an array of string or numeric values (the topic of collections will be covered in greater detail in the chapter entitled *"Creating 2D, 3D, and Jagged Arrays in C#"*).

Consider, for example, the following *foreach* loop construct:

```
string[] myColors = ["red", "green", "yellow", "orange", "blue"];

foreach (string color in myColors)
{
    Console.WriteLine("{0} ", color);
}
```

The loop begins by stating that the current item will be assigned to a constant named *color*. We then tell the statement that it is to iterate through all the elements in the *myColors* collection. The loop's body sends a message to the console panel indicating the current value assigned to the *color* constant.

As we will see in the *"Creating 2D, 3D, and Jagged Arrays in C#"* chapter, the *foreach* loop is particularly beneficial when working with collections such as arrays and dictionaries.

11.9 Take the knowledge test

Click the link below or scan the QR code to test your knowledge and understanding of C# looping:

https://www.answertopia.com/3xzv

11.10 Summary

Looping control flow is a fundamental feature found in most programming languages used to perform tasks that must be executed multiple times. In this chapter, we have covered the C# *for* and *foreach* statements and how they are utilized to execute tasks a specified number of times. Additionally, we have explored nested loops and explained how to manage loop behavior using the *break* and *continue* statements.

Chapter 12

12. C# Looping with do and while Statements

With the topic of constructing loops using the C# *for* statement covered, this chapter aims to introduce two more looping options: the *while* and *do ... while* constructs.

The C# *for* loop described in the previous chapter works well when you know in advance how many times a particular task needs to be repeated in a program. However, there will be instances where code needs to be repeated until a specific condition is met, with no way of knowing how many repetitions will be needed to meet those criteria. While it is possible to achieve this with a *for* loop containing a *break* statement, C# provides a better alternative in the form of the *while* loop (yet another construct inherited by C# from the C Programming Language).

12.1 The C# while loop

Essentially, the *while* loop repeats a set of tasks until a specified condition is met. The *while* loop syntax is defined as follows:

```
while (<condition>) {
    // C# statements go here
}
```

In the above example, <condition> is an expression that will return either true or false, and the *// C# statements go here* comment represents the C# code to be executed while the condition expression continues to evaluate to true. For example:

```
int myCount = 0;


while ( myCount < 100 ) {
    myCount++;
}


Console.WriteLine($"myCount = {myCount}");
```

In the above example, the *while* expression will evaluate whether the *myCount* variable is less than 100. If it is already greater than 100, the code in the braces is skipped, and the loop exits without performing any tasks.

If, on the other hand, *myCount* is not greater than 100, the code in the braces is executed, and the loop returns to the *while* statement and repeats the evaluation of *myCount*. This process repeats until the value of *myCount* exceeds 100, at which point the loop exits.

12.2 C# do … while loops

It is often helpful to think of the *do ... while* loop as an inverted *while* loop. The *while* loop evaluates an expression before executing the code in the loop's body. The code is not executed if the expression evaluates to false on the first check. The *do ... while* loop, on the other hand, is provided for situations where you know that the code contained in the loop's body will always need to be executed at least once. For example, you may want to keep stepping through the items in an array until a specific item is found. You know that you have to at least check the first item in the array to have any hope of finding the entry you need. The syntax for the *do ... while* loop is as follows:

```
do
{
    // C# statements here
} while (<conditional expression>);
```

In the *do ... while* example below, the loop will continue until the value of a variable named *i* equals 0:

```
int i = 10;

do {
    i--;
    Console.WriteLine($"i = {i}");
} while (i > 0);
```

12.3 Breaking from loops

As with the *for* loop, it is also possible to exit from a *while* or *do ... while* loop at any time using the *break* statement. When the execution path encounters a *while* statement, the looping will stop, and execution will proceed to the code immediately following the loop. In the following example, the loop is coded to exit when the value of *i* matches the value of *j*:

```
int i = 0;
int j = 5;

while (i < 100)
{
     i++;
     Console.WriteLine($"i = {i}");
     if (i == j)
            break;
}
```

As with breaking from *for* loops, it is essential to note that in the case of nested *while* and *do ... while* loops, the *while* statement only exits the current loop, leaving the outer loop to continue executing (and most likely once again executing the inner loop).

12.4 The continue statement

The *continue* statement skips all remaining code statements in a loop and returns execution to the top of the loop.

In the following example, the WriteLine() method is only called when the value of variable *i* is an even number (i.e., divisible by 2 with no remainder):

```
int i = 1;

while (i < 20) {
    i++;
    if ((i % 2) != 0)
        continue;
```

```
        Console.WriteLine("i = " + i);
}
```

The *continue* statement in the above example will skip the WriteLine() call unless the value of *i* can be divided by 2 with no remainder. If the *continue* statement is triggered, execution will skip to the top of the *while* loop, and the statements in the body of the loop will be repeated (until the value of *i* exceeds 19).

12.5 Take the knowledge test

Click the link below or scan the QR code to test your knowledge and understanding of C# do-while looping:

https://www.answertopia.com/t2ji

12.6 Summary

The C# *do* and *while* statements are versatile tools for performing a task repeatedly until a specific condition is met, such as an arithmetic operation achieving the desired outcome or data arriving on a network port. When used independently, the *while* loop checks if the criteria have been met before executing the first loop iteration, thus allowing the loop to be skipped entirely. On the other hand, the *do ... while* loop is helpful when you know that the loop code needs to be executed at least once before the completion criteria can be met. Both loops support the *break* and *continue* statements.

Chapter 13

13. An Introduction to C# Object-Oriented Programming

So far in this course, we have looked at the basics of programming in C#, such as variable types and control flow. Although writing a functional program using these techniques would be possible, there is much more to becoming a proficient C# programmer. C# is, above all, an object-oriented programming language, and as such, any C# programmer will be expected to create object-oriented applications using this language.

C# provides extensive support for developing object-oriented applications. This chapter will introduce the basic concepts involved in object-oriented programming and then explain the concept as it relates to application development using C#.

13.1 What is an object?

An object is a self-contained module of functionality that can be easily used and re-used as the building blocks for a software application.

Objects consist of data variables (*properties*) and functions (*methods*) that can be accessed and called on the object to perform tasks. These are collectively referred to as *members*.

13.2 What is a class?

A class is like a blueprint or an architect's drawing that describes what an object will look like when it is created. It defines the methods that the object will have and the variables that it will contain. Essentially, a class determines the attributes and behavior of an object.

13.3 Creating the ObjectDemo project

Launch VS Code, and open your "C# Essentials" workspace folder. Press Cmd-Shift-P to display the Command Palette and select the *.NET: New Project...* command, as illustrated below:

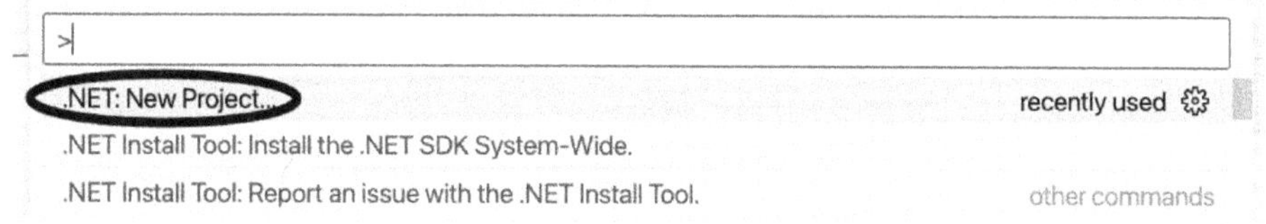

Figure 13-1

Select the Console App option from the template list, name the project ObjectDemo when prompted, and press the Enter key to confirm the selection:

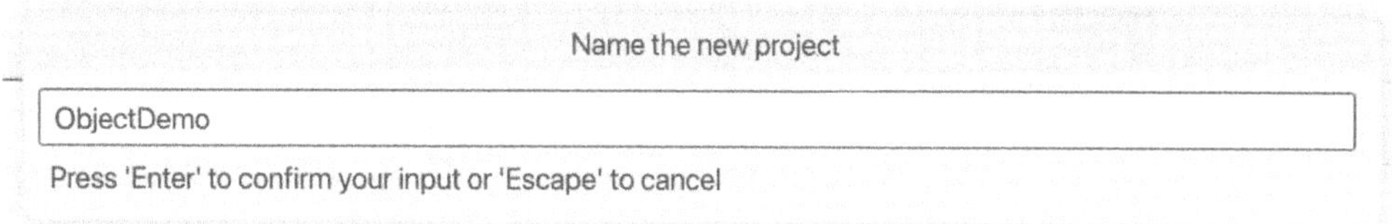

Figure 13-2

Accept the default workspace folder followed by the option to create the new project:

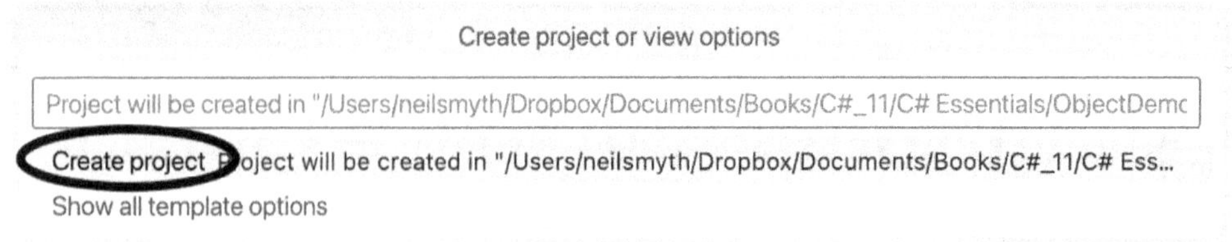

Figure 13-3

Select the Explorer option from the action bar (marked A in Figure 13-4 below) and confirm that the ObjectDemo project is now listed in the workspace folder (B):

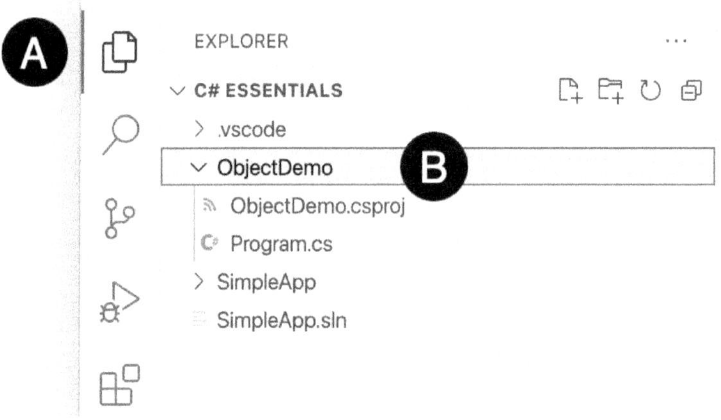

Figure 13-4

13.4 Declaring a C# class

Before an object can be instantiated, we first need to define the class blueprint for the object. In this chapter, we will create a Bank Account class to demonstrate the concepts of C# object-oriented programming. The first step is to use the Solution Explorer to add a new class file to our project. The Solution Explorer is located at the bottom of the Explorer panel as shown in Figure 13-5:

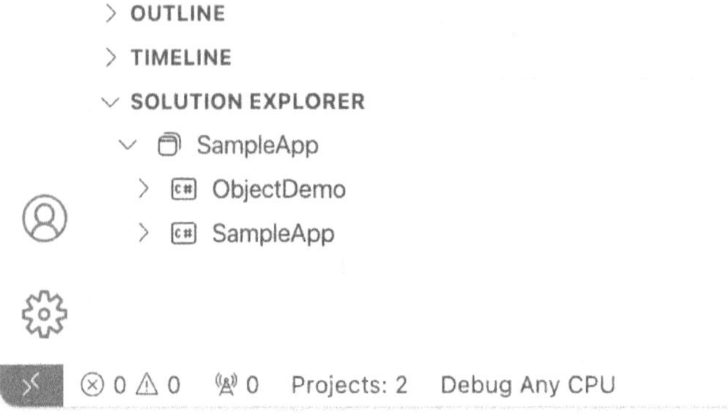

Figure 13-5

Within the Solution Explorer, hover the mouse pointer over the ObjectDemo entry to display the new file and folder buttons:

Figure 13-6

Clicking the Add New File... button will display the Add New File palette as shown in Figure 13-7. Within the palette, select the Class option:

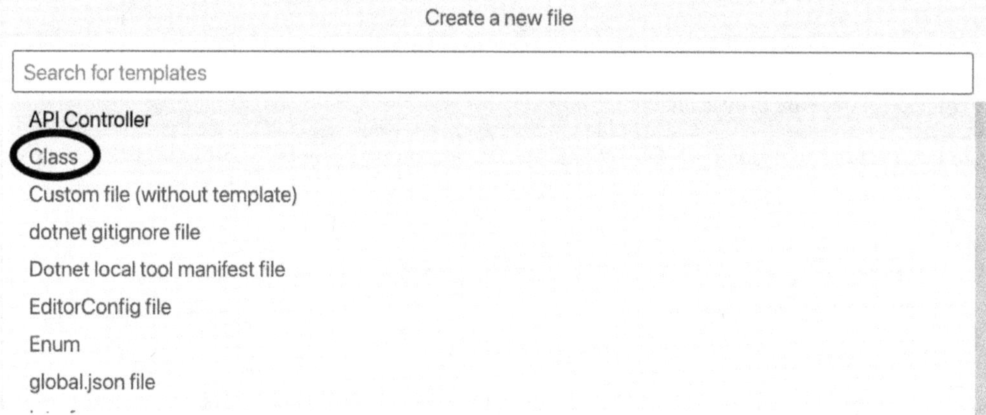

Figure 13-7

When prompted, name the class *BankAccount* before pressing Enter to create the file. The new file will automatically load into the editor, where it will read as follows:

```
using System;

namespace ObjectDemo;

public class BankAccount
{

}
```

13.5 Access modifiers

When VS Code generated our BankAccount class, it declared using the *public* access modifier. Access modifiers control whether the class can be accessed from code elsewhere in the project and can be applied to a variety of types in C#, including classes, methods, members, properties, and fields. C# supports the following access modifiers:

- **public** - There are no restriction on access.

- **protected** - Access is only available from within the containing class or derivatives of the class.
- **private** - Access is only available from within the containing class.
- **file** - Access is only available within the containing source file.
- **internal** - Access is only available to code within the current assembly (typically the code that makes up the compiled executable or library) in which the class is declared.
- **protected internal** - Access is only available to code within the current assembly or derivatives of the containing class.
- **private protected** - Access is only available within the containing class or derivatives within the current assembly.

13.6 Creating C# class members

Class members, fields, or properties are essentially variables and methods embedded in the class (the concept of methods is covered later in the chapter). Members can be *public*, *private*, or *protected.*

Public members can be accessed from outside the object and visible in classes derived from the current class. Private members can only be accessed by methods contained in the class and are not accessible to derived classes. Protected classes are only available to derived classes.

This is the key to *data encapsulation*. Object-oriented programming convention dictates that data should be encapsulated in the class and accessed and set only through the class's methods (typically called *getters* and *setters*).

When implementing data encapsulation, it is important to understand the difference between *fields* and *properties* within C# class declarations.

13.7 Fields vs. properties

A class member directly declared as a variable is called a *field*. In the following class, for example, the *firstname* variable is declared as a field:

```
public class MyClass {
    public string firstname = ""; // This is a field
}
```

This is referred to as a *public field*. When declared this way, code outside the class can directly access and change this variable.

Object-oriented programming guidelines, however, suggest that fields should generally be protected from direct access (known as *private fields*). In C#, this is achieved by declaring a *property*, which, in turn, provides access to the underlying private field.

A property is provided with a name and declares special *get* and *set* methods (referred to as *accessor methods*), which are used to provide access to the underlying field using the following syntax:

```
public string <property name> {
     get {
         return <field name>;
     }
     set {
         <field name> = value;
```

```
    }
}
```

The code of the *get* method returns the value assigned to the field. The *set* method, on the other hand, is passed a variable named *value* that can be assigned to the field.

Using this approach, we can now implement a property to encapsulate our *firstname* field:

```
public class MyClass
{
    private string _firstname = "";

    public string FirstName {
        get {
            return _firstname;
        }
        set {
            _firstname = value;
        }
    }
}
```

When a field is associated with a property, the field should be declared as being private, and the name is generally prefixed with an underscore (_).

A more concise approach to declaring accessors is to use the lambda operator (=>) to assign get and set expressions (the topic of Lambdas will be covered in the *"C# Anonymous Methods, Lambdas, and Local Functions"* chapter):

```
public string <property name> {
     get => <field name>;
     set => <field name> = value;
}
```

Using the above approach, we can simplify our MyClass example as follows:

```
public class MyClass
{
    private string _firstname = "";

    public string FirstName {
        get => _firstname;
        set => _firstname = value;
    }
}
```

Whether or not to encapsulate all fields within properties and have no public fields is a matter of personal preference in terms of how rigidly you want to adhere to object-oriented programming conventions. You will see examples of both approaches even in Microsoft's C# reference documents. For the sake of brevity, we will use public fields in many examples in this book.

13.8 Adding members to the BankAccount class

We can now extend our BankAccount class to add fields to hold the account name and number. True to the concept of data encapsulation, we will be making these fields private and using properties to provide access:

```
.
.
namespace ObjectDemo;

public class BankAccount
{
    private string _accountName = "";
    private int _accountNumber = 0;

    public string AccountName
    {
        get => _accountName;
        set => _accountName = value;
    }

    public int AccountNumber
    {
        get => _accountNumber;
        set => _accountNumber = value;
    }
}
```

With some fields and properties added to our class, we need to briefly examine a few additional data member types and learn how to create object instances from the class.

13.9 Static, read-only, and const data members

In addition to the data member types we have looked at so far, C# also supports several additional member types.

C# *static member* types (also called *class properties*) store data values common to all object instances of the class. For example, all bank customers would earn the same interest rate on a savings account. Therefore, an *interestRate* member would be declared static since it is shared across all object instances of the class. Static members are declared using the *static* keyword. For example:

```
public class BankAccount
{
   private static int interestRate;
}
```

Static members are accessed through the class, not through the object. For example, we would change the *interestRate* member for all object instances by referencing the BankAccount class as follows:

```
BankAccount.interestRate = 10;
```

For data members that must not be modified the *const* and *readonly* keywords are provided by C#. Both achieve the same objective of preventing the value assigned to a data member from being changed after it has been declared. The value of a *const* or *readonly* member must be assigned at creation time:

```
public readonly int daysInWeek = 7;
```

13.10 Instantiating an object from a C# class

Creating an object from the class 'blueprint' is called *instantiation*. The first step is to create an object variable of the required object type. An instance of the object is then created using the *new* keyword and assigned to the object variable:

```
BankAccount custAccount;
custAccount = new BankAccount();
```

It is also possible to declare the object variable and assign the object in a single statement:

```
BankAccount custAccount = new BankAccount();
```

Alternatively, since we have declared *custAccount* as being of type BankAccount, we can let the compiler infer that we are requesting an new BankAccount instance as follows:

```
BankAccount custAccount = new();
```

Edit the *Program.cs* file and add the following code:

```
using ObjectDemo;

BankAccount custAccount = new();
```

Having created an instance of our BankAccount class the next step is to learn how to access the members of the class.

13.11 Accessing C# object members

Now that we know how to write a class and instantiate objects from it, we need to know how to access its members.

First, you will recall that we declared some members as being public and others as being private. The public methods are fully accessible from outside the object. This is achieved using something called *dot notation.*

Dot notation is a mechanism by which object members may be accessed by specifying the object and member names separated by a dot (.). For example, to access the *accountName* member of an object named *custAccount* we would reference this member using custAccount.accountName.

Modify the *Program.cs* file as follows to access the public member properties of the BankAccount object using dot notation:

```
BankAccount custAccount = new();

custAccount.AccountName = "John Smith";
custAccount.AccountNumber = 53211;

Console.WriteLine($"Customer Name is {custAccount.AccountName}");
Console.WriteLine($"Account Number = {custAccount.AccountNumber}");
```

After creating an instance of our BankAccount class, the above code assigns values to two private fields via our object's AccountName and AccountNumber properties. The code then references these properties to display the customer name and account number values.

Run the app and check that the output reads as follows:

```
Customer Name is John Smith
```

```
Account Number = 53211
```

In the above example, we created the *custAccount* object, then used dot notation to assign a customer name and account number to the instance. When properties are initialized immediately after object creation, the code can be simplified as follows to perform the object instantiation and property initialization in a single operation:

```
BankAccount custAccount = new()
{
    AccountName = "John Smith",
    AccountNumber = 53211
};
```

13.12 Adding methods to a C# class

Class methods are essentially code routines that can be called to perform specific tasks within the class's context.

Methods come in two forms: *static methods* (also called *class methods*) and *instance methods*. Static methods operate at the class level, such as creating a new class instance. On the other hand, instance methods operate only on the instances of a class (for example, performing an arithmetic operation on two member variables and returning the result).

Instance methods are declared within the opening and closing braces of the class to which they belong and are declared using the standard C# method declaration syntax.

Static methods are declared like instance methods, except that the *static* keyword precedes the declaration.

For example, edit the BankAccount class and add a method to display the customer's name as follows:

```
public class BankAccount
{
    private string _accountName = "";
    private int _accountNumber = 0;
.
.
    public void DisplayName()
    {
        Console.WriteLine($"Customer name is {AccountName}");
    }
}
```

The method above is an instance method, so the *static* keyword does not precede it and can be called as follows:

```
BankAccount custAccount = new()
{
    AccountName = "John Smith",
    AccountNumber = 53211
};
.
.
custAccount.DisplayName();
Console.WriteLine($"Account Number = {custAccount.AccountNumber}");
```

When designing the BankAccount class, it might be helpful to call a static method on the class itself to identify the maximum allowable balance that class instances can store. This would enable an application to identify whether the BankAccount class is suitable for storing details of a new customer without creating a class instance. We will name this method GetMaxBalance() and implement it as follows:

```
public class BankAccount {
.
.
    public static double GetMaxBalance()
    {
        return(10000000.00);
    }
}
```

With the method declared, it can be called directly on the class without the need to create an instance as follows:

```
double maxBalance = BankAccount.GetMaxBalance();
Console.WriteLine($"Maximum allowed balance = ${maxBalance}");

BankAccount custAccount = new()
{
.
.
```

Running the app should produce the following output:

```
Maximum allowed balance = $10000000
Customer name is John Smith
Account Number = 53211
```

Now that we have looked at method class members, the next task is to look at two special class methods: *constructors* and *finalizers*.

13.13 C# constructors

Despite the grand-sounding names, C# class constructors and finalizers are nothing more than methods that get called when an object is instantiated and destroyed. The constructor is particularly useful for allowing initialization values to be passed through to an object at creation time. Let's say that we would like to be able to initialize the _accountName and _accountNumber members at the point that we initialize the *custAccount* object. To do so, we need to declare a constructor.

Constructors are declared the same way as other methods with the exception that the name of the method must match the class name. For example, add a constructor to our BankAccount class as follows:

```
public class BankAccount
{
    private string _accountName;
    private int _accountNumber;

    // Constructor
    public BankAccount(string accountName, int accountNumber)
    {
        _accountName = accountName;
        _accountNumber = accountNumber;
    }
```

```
.
.
}
```

The constructor can be used to initialize these members at the point that the instance is created:

```
BankAccount custAccount = new BankAccount("Fred Wilson", 123456);

custAccount.DisplayName();
```

The type of constructor outlined above is particularly useful when tasks need to be performed in addition to assigning values to properties. For example, the BankAccount constructor might include some logic to catch an empty customer name string:

```
public BankAccount(string accountName, int accountNumber)
{
    if (accountName == "")
        _accountName = "Anonymous";
    else
        _accountName = accountName;

    _accountNumber = accountNumber;
}
```

A class can contain multiple constructors, each with a unique set of parameters. Consider the following changes to the BankAccount class definition:

```
public class BankAccount
{
    private string _accountName;
    private int _accountNumber;
    private bool _isActive = false;

    // Constructor
    public BankAccount(string accountName, int accountNumber)
    {
        _accountName = accountName;
        _accountNumber = accountNumber;
    }

    public BankAccount(string accountName, int accountNumber, bool isActive)
    {
        _accountName = accountName;
        _accountNumber = accountNumber;
        _isActive = isActive;
    }

    public bool IsActive {
        get => _isActive;
        set => _isActive = value;
```

```
    }
.
.
```

With these changes, BankAccount class instances may be created using either constructor:

```
BankAccount custAccount = new("John Smith", 53211);
BankAccount custAccount2 = new("John Smith", 53211, true);
```

13.14 C# primary constructors

When a constructor's sole purpose is to assign provided parameters to properties with no additional actions, a *primary constructor* is recommended. Primary constructors are declared by placing the parameters after the class name and assigning them to the private variables. For example:

```
public class BankAccount(string accountName, int accountNumber)
{
    private string _accountName = accountName;
    private int _accountNumber = accountNumber;

    // Constructor
    public BankAccount(string accountName, int accountNumber)
    {
        _accountName = accountName;
        _accountNumber = accountNumber;
    }
```

13.15 C# finalizers

Finalizers are used to clean up any resources a class object uses when the object is destroyed. Unlike constructors, which can be triggered from code using the *new* keyword, there is no way to explicitly call a finalizer (for example, there is no delete equivalent to the *new* keyword). Instead, the finalizer will be called when the runtime system decides the object instance is no longer needed. All the programmer can be sure of is that the finalizer will be called at some time between when the code no longer needs the object and the point that the application terminates.

Finalizers are defined in the same way as constructors, with the exception that they cannot be public and the name is preceded by the tilde character (~):

```
// Finalizer
~BankAccount() {
    // Code to perform clean-up
}
```

13.16 The "this" keyword

When constructing classes in C#, you may encounter situations where a property that is local to a method or the name assigned to the method parameter conflicts with a class property. This is particularly common when using public fields within class declarations.

Take, for example, the following sample class in which the parameter names for the initializer match those of the public fields:

```
class DemoClass
{
```

```
    public string name;
    public int age;

    public DemoClass(string name, int age)
    {
        name = name;
        age = age;
    }
}
```

The following code creates a DemoClass instance and initializes it with name and age values:

```
DemoClass demo = new("Mark", 37);
Console.WriteLine($"{demo.name} is {demo.age} is years old.");
```

When the above code runs, there will be no name and the age will be 0 even though age was set to 37 when the class instance was created. In addition, the compiler will issue a warning which reads:

```
warning CS1717: Assignment made to same variable; did you mean to assign
something else?
```

The problem here is that the compiler doesn't know which *name* and *age* variables are being referenced in the following initializer code:

```
public DemoClass(string name, int age) {
    name = name;
    age = age;
}
```

To resolve this problem, we need a way to tell the compiler that the method parameter values are to be assigned to the corresponding public field values. We can do this using the *this* keyword. In this context, the *this* keyword represents the current class instance. To differentiate the conflicting *name* and *age* variables, we need to use the *this* keyword as follows:

```
public DemoClass(string name, int age) {
    this.name = name;
    this.age = age;
}
```

Now we not only no longer see the compiler's warning messages but see Mark's name and correct age.

13.17 Take the knowledge test

Click the link below or scan the QR code to test your knowledge and understanding of C# object-oriented programming:

https://www.answertopia.com/cnbw

13.18 Summary

Object-oriented programming languages like C# promote the creation of classes to encourage code reuse and data encapsulation. In this chapter, we have covered the fundamental concepts of classes and instances within C# and explained concepts such as class members, constructors, finalizers, properties, fields, and methods.

Chapter 14

14. C# Methods

The previous chapter began the introduction to object-oriented programming in C# and included the use of methods declared within classes. This chapter will explore C# methods in more detail, including how they are declared and called, passing arguments, and returning results. The topic of passing arguments by reference and value will also be explained.

C# methods are vital to writing well-structured and efficient code. They provide a way to organize programs while avoiding code repetition. In this chapter, we will examine how methods are declared and used within C#.

14.1 What is a method?

A method is a named block of code that can be called upon to perform a specific task. It can be passed data on which to perform the task and return results to the code that called it. For example, if a particular arithmetic calculation needs to be performed in a C# program, the code to perform the arithmetic can be placed in a method. The method can be programmed to accept the values on which the arithmetic is to be performed (referred to as *parameters*) and return the calculation result. At any point in the program code where the calculation is required, the method is called and passed values as *arguments*, and the result is returned.

14.2 Methods vs. functions

You may have heard about or used functions if you are familiar with other programming languages. Generally, functions are declared the same way as methods and fulfill the same purpose. The difference is that methods must be declared within a class, while functions are declared outside of a class. In terms of C#, it is only possible to declare methods within a class, and the concept of functions does not exist.

14.3 Parameter or argument?

The terms parameter and argument are often used interchangeably when discussing methods. However, there is a subtle difference. The values a method can accept when it is called are called parameters. When the method is called and passed those values, they are referred to as arguments.

14.4 How to declare a C# function

A C# function is declared using the following syntax:

```
<access> <return type> <method name>(<para type> <para name>, <para type> <para name>, ...){
    // Method code
}
```

Explanations of the various fields of the function declaration are as follows:

- **<access>** – Defines the level of access to the method from other parts of the code. Valid values are public, private, or protected, as explained in the previous chapter.
- **<return type>** – The data type of the result returned by the function. If the function does not return a result, then this is set to *void*.
- **<method name>** – The name assigned to the method. This is the name by which the method will be referenced when it is called from within the application code.

- **<para type>** – The type of the corresponding parameter.
- **<para name>** – The name by which the parameter is referenced in the method code.
- **Method code** – The code statements of the method that perform the work.

As an example, the following method takes no parameters, returns no result, and displays a message:

```
public void sayHello() {
    Console.WriteLine("Hello");
}
```

The following sample function, on the other hand, takes an int and a string as parameters and returns a string result:

```
public string BuildMessage(string name, int count) {
    return($"{name}, you are customer number {count}");
}
```

14.5 Creating the MethodDemo project

Launch VS Code, open your "C# Essentials" workspace folder and create a new .NET Console App project named MethodDemo.

14.6 Declaring a C# class file

Following the steps in the *"An Introduction to C# Object-Oriented Programming"* chapter, use the Solutions Explorer to add a new class file named Demo to the MethodDemo project. Once you have added the class file, modify it as follows to add a method:

```
using System;

namespace MethodDemo;

public class Demo
{
    public void SayHello()
    {
        Console.WriteLine("Hello");
    }
}
```

14.7 Calling a C# method

Once declared, C# methods are called on class instances using dot notation using the following syntax:

```
<instance>.<function name>(<arg1>, <arg2>, ... )
```

Each argument passed through to a method must match the parameters the method is configured to accept. For example, to call the above example method named SayHello(), which takes no parameters and returns no value, we need to modify the *Program.cs* file as follows:

```
using MethodDemo;

Demo demo = new();
demo.SayHello();
```

When the app runs, the "Hello" message will appear in the terminal.

14.8 Handling return values

The SayHello() method definition included the *void* keyword to indicate that it did not return a result value. Next, add a method named BuildMessage() to the Demo class which accepts two parameters and returns a string result as follows:

```
public class Demo
{
    public void SayHello()
    {
        Console.WriteLine("Hello");
    }

    public string BuildMessage(string name, int count)
    {
        return ($"Hello {name}, you are visitor number {count}.");
    }
}
```

In the above code, we placed parentheses around the return value as follows:

```
return ($"Hello {name}, you are visitor number { count}");
```

These parentheses are optional, so the following is also a valid use of the return statement:

```
return $"Hello {name}, you are visitor number {count}.";
```

Return to the *Program.cs* file and add code to call the new method:

```
Demo demo = new();
string message = demo.BuildMessage("Bill", 10);
Console.WriteLine(message);
```

In the above example, we created a new variable named *message* and used the assignment operator (=) to store the method's result before writing it to the console. When the app runs, the following output should appear in the terminal:

```
Hello Bill, you are visitor number 10.
```

14.9 Passing arguments to a method

Several options are available when calling a method that is expecting arguments. One option, as demonstrated above, is to pass the arguments in the order in which they are declared in the method declaration:

```
string message = demo.BuildMessage("Bill Gates", 10);
```

When calling a method in this way, the arguments must be passed in the order in which the parameters are declared in the method. Passing arguments to a method using this technique can also make it difficult to understand the purpose of each argument. Both of these issues can be resolved using named arguments.

14.9.1 Named arguments

Using named arguments involves referencing the parameter names assigned in the method declaration when making calls. For example:

```
demo.BuildMessage(name: "Steve", count: 30);
```

Since ordering is not important when using named arguments, the following is also a valid call:

```
demo.BuildMessage(count: 30, name: "Steve");
```

Make the following changes to the *Program.cs* file to see named arguments in action:

```
Demo demo = new();
string message = demo.BuildMessage(name: "Bill", count: 10);
Console.WriteLine(message);

message = demo.BuildMessage(count: 30, name: "Steve");
Console.WriteLine(message);
```

As demonstrated in the code above, the ordering of the arguments no longer matters when making the method call. It is also easier to understand the purpose of each argument being passed to the method.

14.9.2 Optional arguments

C# arguments can be made optional by designating a default parameter value to be used if the value is not provided as an argument when the method is called. This involves assigning the default value to the parameter when the method is declared. When working with optional arguments, the only requirement is to place the optional parameters after any mandatory parameters in the method declaration.

Modify the BuildMessage() method as follows so that the string "Customer" is used as the default if a customer name is not provided when the method is called:

```
public class Demo
{
    public void SayHello()
    {
        Console.WriteLine("Hello");
    }

    public string BuildMessage(int count, string name = "Customer")
    {
        return $"Hello {name}, you are visitor number {count}.";
    }
}
```

After making the change to the method, try calling it without a name argument:

```
Demo demo = new();

string message = demo.BuildMessage(count: 10);
Console.WriteLine(message);
```

When the app runs, the following output will appear with "Customer" substituted for the name:

```
Hello Customer, you are visitor number 10.
```

14.10 Handling variable numbers of arguments

So far we have looked at method examples that accept a fixed number of arguments when called. C# also provides a way to configure a method to accept a variable number of arguments. This involves placing the arguments in a List collection and handling it using the *params* keyword. The C# List class allows multiple items to be grouped within a single object and will be covered in the *"C# List Collections"* chapter. Suppose that we need a method that will accept an unspecified number of string arguments. Using the *params* keyword, we could declare the method as follows:

```
public void GreetGuests(params List<string> guests)
{
    foreach (var guest in guests) {
        Console.WriteLine($"Welcome, {guest}");
    }
}
```

When we call the GreetGuests() method, we can pass it a List instance containing any number of guest names without making changes to the GreetGuests() method:

```
List<string> names = ["John", "Paul", "George"];
demo.GreetGuests(names);

names = ["Mark", "Robert"];
demo.GreetGuests(names);
```

A *params* parameter can be combined with other method parameters, for example:

```
public void GreetGuests(int groupId, params List<string> guests)
{
.
.
}
```

A method can accept only one *params* argument, which must be positioned at the end of the parameter list.

14.11 C# in, out, and ref parameter modifiers

When an argument is passed to a method, it is passed as a *value*. Suppose the code contains an int variable named *myVar*, to which the value 10 is assigned. The *myVar* variable is then passed to a method named DoSomething(). In this scenario, only a copy of the value 10 is passed to the method with no connection to the original *myVar* variable. Consequently, any changes to the value from within the method will not be reflected in the original variable.

Add the following method to the Demo class to demonstrate this effect in action:

```
public class Demo {
.
.
    public void DoSomething(int myVar) {
        myVar = 10;
    }
}
```

Next, modify the *Program.cs* file as follows:

```
int myVar = 20;
Demo demo = new();

Console.WriteLine($"Before method call myVar = {myVar}");
demo.DoSomething(myVar);
Console.WriteLine($"After method call myVar = {myVar}");
```

The code above declares a variable and assigns it a value of 20. Before calling the method, the current value of *myVar* is displayed. The variable is then passed as an argument to the DoSomething() method, where it is assigned a value of 10. When the DoSomething() method returns, the value assigned to the *myVar* variable is output again.

Run the app and verify the value assigned to the *myVar* variable was not changed by the DoSomething() method:

```
Before method call myVar = 20
After method call myVar = 20
```

To allow the value assigned to the variable to be changed within the method, we need to pass the variable by *reference.*

Passing by reference means that instead of passing the underlying value, we are passing a reference to the location in memory where the variable stores its value. Any changes made within the method will be made to the variable's value.

A variable is passed by reference using the *ref* modifier both when declaring the parameter in the method and when calling the method, as shown below:

```
// Demo.cs
public class Demo {
.
.
    public void DoSomething(ref int myVar) {
        myVar = 10;
    }
}

// Program.cs
Console.WriteLine($"Before method call myVar = {myVar}");
demo.DoSomething(ref myVar);
Console.WriteLine($"After method call myVar = {myVar}");
```

The output from running the app shows that the value assigned to *myVar* changes from 20 to 10 after the method call:

```
Before method call myVar = 20
After method call myVar = 10
```

Another modifier available when calling methods is the *out* keyword. Whether the variable value is changed within the method is optional when using the *ref* modifier. To force the change to the variable within the method, use the *out* modifier instead of the *ref.*

The *out* modifier is generally used to force the method to initialize a variable when it is null at the point it is passed. For example:

```
// Demo.cs
.
.
public void DoSomething(out string myVar)
{
    myVar = "Hello";
```

```
}

// Program.cs
string myVar;
Demo demo = new();

demo.DoSomething(out myVar);
Console.WriteLine($"After method call myVar = {myVar}");
```

The final modifier to be covered is the *in* modifier. This modifier also sends the variable to the method by reference but prevents that reference from being changed from within the method. The following code change, for example, will generate a syntax error because *myVar* is now a read-only variable:

```
// Demo.cs
.
.
public void DoSomething(in string myVar)
{
    myVar = "Hello"; // Syntax error - readonly variable
}

// Program.cs
.
.
demo.DoSomething(in myVar);
.
.
```

14.12 Take the knowledge test

Click the link below or scan the QR code to test your knowledge and understanding of C# methods:

https://www.answertopia.com/r67i

14.13 Summary

C# methods are self-contained units of code that perform a specific task. They help structure code and facilitate code reuse. This chapter discussed C# methods and explained how to create and invoke them. We also described how to add parameters to a method and differentiate between named and optional arguments. Finally, we learned when to use the in, out, and ref parameter modifiers and the difference between passing arguments to a method by value and reference.

Chapter 15

15. C# Delegates

This chapter will continue exploring C# methods by introducing the concepts of C# delegates, including what they are and how to use them.

15.1 What is a delegate?

Before we start exploring C# delegates, it first helps to understand the concept of method signatures. When a method is declared, the parameters it accepts and the result type it returns make up the method's signature. The signature of the following method indicates that it accepts a string value as a parameter and returns an integer:

```
public int GetLength(string value) {
.
.
}
```

The following method performs an entirely different task but has the identical signature as the above GetLength() method:

```
public int CustomerCount(string customer) {
.
.
}
```

A C# delegate is a variable that stores a reference to a method. If you are familiar with C or C++ programming, delegates are similar to function pointers.

Once declared, the delegate can be changed to point to any method that matches the delegate's method signature.

15.2 Declaring a delegate

Delegates are declared using the *delegate* keyword and the following syntax:

```
delegate <returntype> <delegatename> (<parameters>);
```

To declare a delegate that matches our two example methods (a string parameter and an integer return type), we would write the following:

```
public delegate string MyDelegate (string s);
```

15.3 Using delegates

With a delegate declared, we can use it to store references to methods. Delegate instances are created using the *new* keyword, passing through the method to be referenced, for example:

```
public delegate string MyDelegate (string s);

MyDelegate delegate1 = new MyDelegate(GetLength);
MyDelegate delegate2 = new MyDelegate(CustomerCount);
```

In the above code, we have created two delegate instances, each pointing to one of our example methods. Once declared, these can be called just like any other method:

```
var strlen = delegate1("This is some text");
var count = delegate2("Robert Addison");
```

15.4 Creating the DelegateDemo project

Launch VS Code, open your "C# Essentials" workspace folder, and create a new .NET Console App project named DelegateDemo.

15.5 A C# delegate example

In this example, we will create a delegate called StringConverter. Begin by editing the *Program.cs* file as follows:

```
namespace DelegateDemo
{
    internal class Program
    {
        delegate string StringConverter(string value);

        static string LowerCase(string value)
        {
             Console.Write("Converting to lowercase > ");
             return value.ToLower();
        }

        static string UpperCase(string value)
        {
            Console.Write("Converting to uppercase > ");
            return value.ToUpper();
        }

        static void Main(string[] args)
        {
        }
    }
}
```

The above changes declare a delegate named StringConverter that can be used to reference any method that accepts and returns a string value. Next, we declared two methods matching this signature, LowerCase() and UpperCase(). The next step is to add code the Main() method to use these delegates:

```
static void Main(string[] args)
{
    StringConverter converter1 = new(LowerCase);
    StringConverter converter2 = new(UpperCase);

    var lower = converter1("This is some TEXT");
    Console.WriteLine(lower);

    var upper = converter2("tHis IS sOmE TExt");
    Console.WriteLine(upper);
```

```
}
```

The Main() method creates two delegate instances, each referencing one of the two methods. These methods are then called via the delegates, and the resulting strings are displayed in the console:

```
Converting to lowercase > this is some text
Converting to uppercase > THIS IS SOME TEXT
```

Since the delegate is a variable, a different method may be assigned at any time.

In the above example, converter1 and converter2 are single cast delegates in that they reference only one method each. It is also possible to create multicast delegates.

15.6 Multicast delegates

A multicast delegate contains more than one delegate, allowing it to reference multiple methods. Multicast delegates are created by combining existing delegates using the + operator.

The following changes to our Main() method create a delegate named multicast comprising both converter1 and converter2:

```
static void Main(string[] args)
{
    StringConverter converter1 = new(LowerCase);
    StringConverter converter2 = new(UpperCase);
    StringConverter multicast = converter1 + converter2;

    var result = multicast("This is some TEXT");
    Console.WriteLine(result);
}
```

When the code is executed, we will see from the console output that both the LowerCase() and UpperCase() methods were called via the single multicast delegate call:

```
Converting to lowercase > Converting to uppercase > THIS IS SOME TEXT
```

Delegates can be removed from a multicast delegate using the '-' operator. The following changes adapt the above example to remove converter2 from multicast after the first call:

```
static void Main(string[] args)
{
    StringConverter converter1 = new(LowerCase);
    StringConverter converter2 = new(UpperCase);

    StringConverter multicast = converter1 + converter2;

    var result = multicast("This is some TEXT");
    Console.WriteLine(result);

    multicast -= converter2;

    result = multicast("AfTeR reMovAL oF converter2");
    Console.WriteLine(result);
}
```

When the code executes, the first call to the delegate results in calls to the LowerCase() and UpperCase() methods. After the removal of converter2 from the multicast delegate, only LowerCase() is called.

```
Converting to lowercase > Converting to uppercase > THIS IS SOME TEXT
Converting to lowercase > after removal of converter2
```

15.7 Passing a delegate to a method

C# delegates have some useful capabilities, one of which is the ability to be passed as arguments to other methods.

If you need a method to accept a delegate as a parameter, declare the parameter type accordingly in the method signature. Suppose we need to write a method that takes as parameters an instance of our StringConverter delegate and a string to be converted. Such a method could be declared as follows:

```
public static void DisplayText(StringConverter converter)
{
    // Code to display text  here
}
```

Make the following changes to fully implement the DisplayText() method and call it from the Main() method:

```
namespace DelegateDemo
{
    internal class Program
    {
        delegate string StringConverter(string value);

.
.
        static void DisplayText(StringConverter converter, string text)
        {
            string result = converter(text);
            Console.WriteLine($"Converted text = {result}");
        }

        static void Main(string[] args)
        {
            StringConverter converter1 = new(LowerCase);
            StringConverter converter2 = new(UpperCase);
.
.
            DisplayText(converter1, "This IS a teST.");
        }
    }
}
```

When the code executes, the following output will appear in the console indicating that the delegate was successfully passed to the DisplayText() method:

```
Converting to lowercase > Converted text = this is a test.
```

15.8 Take the knowledge test

Click the link below or scan the QR code to test your knowledge and understanding of C# delegates:

https://www.answertopia.com/zcfz

15.9 Summary

C# delegates allow us to store references to methods as variables, where the method's signature dictates the variable type. A method's signature is defined by a combination of the parameters it accepts and the type of result it returns. Once a delegate has been declared, it will have the capabilities of many other data types. In particular, delegates allow methods to be passed as arguments to other methods or even returned as a method result. Delegates can contain a single method (single cast) or be combined to create multicast delegates.

Chapter 16

16. C# Anonymous Methods, Lambdas, and Local Functions

In this chapter, you will learn how to use anonymous methods, lambdas, and local functions in C# to write flexible, concise, and reusable code.

16.1 Anonymous methods

Anonymous methods are declared using the *delegate* keyword. Unlike traditional delegates, however, anonymous methods do not reference existing named methods. Instead, the code to be executed is assigned directly to the delegate (a concept referred to as *inline*). When declaring an anonymous method, you will use the following syntax:

```
delegate <returntype> <delegatename> (<parameters>);
```

The differences appear when you assign the code to be executed. The syntax for assigning a block of code to be executed by an anonymous method is as follows:

```
<delegate_type> <delegate_name> = delegate(<parameters>) {
    // Code to be executed
};
```

Using this syntax and taking our LowerCase() method code as an example, we would write code as follows:

```
delegate string StringConverter(string value);

StringConverter converter = delegate(string value)
{
    Console.Write("Converting to lowercase > ");
    return value.ToLower();
};
```

16.2 Creating the LambdaDemo project

To see the above anonymous method declaration in action, launch VS Code, open your "C# Essentials" workspace folder and create a new .NET Console App project named LambdaDemo. Next, modify the *Program.cs* file as follows:

```
namespace LambdaDemo
{
    internal class Program
    {
        delegate string StringConverter(string value);

        static void Main(string[] args)
        {
            StringConverter converter = delegate (string value)
```

```
            {
                Console.Write("Inline conversion to lowercase > ");
                return value.ToLower();
            };
        }
    }
}
```

The above code declares the StringConverter delegate, creates an instance named *converter*, and assigns to it an anonymous method that converts the string argument to lowercase. All that remains is to call the converter and display the result:

```
static void Main(string[] args)
{
    StringConverter converter = delegate (string value)
    {
        Console.Write("Inline conversion to lowercase > ");
        return value.ToLower();
    };

    var result = converter("This is some TEXT");
    Console.WriteLine(result);
}
```

When the above code executes, the following output will appear in the console:

```
Inline conversion to lowercase > this is some text
```

As with standard delegates, you can also pass anonymous methods as arguments to other methods using the syntax outlined in the previous chapter, for example:

```
namespace LambdaDemo
{
    internal class Program
    {
        delegate string StringConverter(string value);

        static void DisplayText(StringConverter converter, string text)
        {
            string result = converter(text);
            Console.WriteLine($"Converted text = { result}");
        }

        static void Main(string[] args)
        {
            StringConverter converter = delegate (string value)
            {
                Console.Write("Inline conversion to lowercase > ");
                return value.ToLower();
            };
```

```
            DisplayText(converter, "This IS a teST.");
        }
    }
}
```

Running the above code will produce the following output:

```
Inline conversion to lowercase > Converted text = this is a test.
```

16.3 Lambdas

You can think of lambdas as anonymous methods that allow code to be written more concisely. As with delegates and anonymous methods, you will first need to declare a variable of type delegate in which to store the lambda reference and to define the return value and parameter types using the following, now familiar, syntax:

```
delegate <returntype> <delegatename> (<parameters>);
```

Lambdas are declared using the => operator. The left side of the operator lists the input parameters, and the right side consists of an expression or code block containing the code to be executed.

C# supports the following types of lambda:

- **Expression lambda** – The lambda body contains a single expression to be executed.
- **Statement lambda** – The lambda body contains a statement block enclosed in braces ({}) containing multiple statements.

The syntax for an expression lambda reads as follows:

```
(input-parameters) => expression
```

When passing a single parameter to a lambda, the parentheses placed around the input parameters in the above syntax are optional.

A statement lambda, on the other hand, uses the following syntax:

```
(input-parameters) => { <statements> };
```

To appreciate the concise nature of lambdas, consider the following slightly modified anonymous method declaration from our *Program.cs* file:

```
delegate string StringConverter(string s);
.
.
StringConverter converter = delegate (string s)
{
    return s.ToLower();
};
```

Using a lambda, we can implement the same behavior as follows:

```
.
.
internal class Program
{
    delegate string StringConverter(string s);
```

```
    static void Main(string[] args)
    {
        StringConverter converter = s => s.ToLower();

        var result = converter("LAMBDA Demo");

        Console.WriteLine(result);
    }
}
```

Before using a lambda, we started with the following code:

```
delegate(string s)
{
    return s.ToLower();
};
```

Using a lambda has allowed us to reduce the original code to the following:

```
s => s.ToLower();
```

In the above lambda example, the left side of the lambda operator indicates that a single parameter named *s* is being passed through to the expression on the right. Notice that we did not need to declare that s is of type string. This is because we have already declared the type in the delegate variable declaration. The expression simply returns the value after converting it to lowercase. Having declared the lambda, we call it just like an anonymous method:

```
var result = converter("LAMBDA Demo");
```

16.4 Passing multiple parameters

Our earlier lambda example used only one input parameter. If you need to pass multiple parameters to a lambda, you can do so by enclosing them in parentheses (()). For example:

```
.
.
delegate string MultiLambda(string s, int i, double d);
.
.
static void Main(string[] args)
{
    MultiLambda sample = (s, i, d) => $"Product = {s}, Count = {i}, Price =
${d}";
.
.
    Console.WriteLine(sample("HDMI Cable", 5, 20.99));
}
```

When the app runs, the product properties will be displayed as follows:

```
Product = HDMI Cable, Count = 5, Price = $20.99
```

16.5 Passing no parameters

Alternately, a lambda that accepts no parameters is declared using empty parentheses:

```
.
.
delegate string SayHello();
.
.
static void Main(string[] args)
{
    SayHello hello = () => "Hello";

    Console.WriteLine(hello());
}
```

16.6 Local functions

Local functions are similar in many ways to lambda expressions with some important differences. Local functions are named methods that are declared within other methods. Like private methods, local functions are not accessible outside the scope of the containing method and do not need to be assigned to delegate variables.

Local functions are declared in the same way as any other C# method. For example, the following is the local function equivalent of our StringConverter lambda:

```
string converter(string s)
{
    return s.ToLower();
}
```

Since the converter function only contains a single expression, we can abbreviate the statement using the => operator:

```
string converter(string s) => s.ToLower();
```

Unlike anonymous methods and lambdas, local functions have direct access to the local variables and values within the containing method's scope.

16.7 Creating the LocalFunctions project

To try out local functions, create a new .NET Console App project in VS Code, and name it LocalFunctions. Once the project has been created, edit the *Program.cs* file so that it reads as follows:

```
namespace LocalFunctions
{
    internal class Program
    {
        static void Main(string[] args)
        {
            ConvertToEuros(10.00);
        }

        private static void ConvertToEuros(double value)
        {
            var exchangeRate = 0.5;

            double USDToEuro(double dollars) => exchangeRate * dollars;
```

```
            var result = USDToEuro(value);
            Console.WriteLine(result);
        }
    }
}
```

The ConvertToEuros() method accepts a dollar amount and returns the equivalent in euros. Within this method, we have declared a local function called USDToEuro() which multiplies the dollar parameter value by the local exchange rate variable and returns the result:

```
double USDToEuro(double dollars) => exchangeRate * dollars;
```

A key point to note in this example is that the local function has access to both the value parameter and the local *exchangeRate* variable, neither of which would have been directly available to a lambda expression.

16.8 Recursive local functions

Local functions can also be called recursively (in other words, a local function can call itself either directly or indirectly). Calculating the factorial of a number is a classic example of recursion. The following code declares a method named FindFactorial() containing a local function named Factorial() which calls itself recursively to identify the factorial of a number:

```
private static int FindFactorial(int value)
{
    int Factorial(int number)
    {
        // Base case
        if (number == 0)
        {
            return 1;
        }

        // Recursive case
        return number * Factorial(number - 1);
    }

    return Factorial(value);
}
```

Add the above method to the *Program.cs* file and call it from the Main() method as follows:

```
static void Main(string[] args)
{
    for (int i=1; i<10; i++)
    {
        var factorial = FindFactorial(i);

        Console.WriteLine($"{i}! = {factorial}");
    }
}
```

When the app runs, it will generate the following output:

```
1! = 1
2! = 2
3! = 6
4! = 24
5! = 120
6! = 720
7! = 5040
8! = 40320
9! = 362880
```

16.9 Lambdas vs. local functions

In general, the choice between lambdas and local functions is a matter of personal coding style, though there are some advantages to using local functions such as direct access to local variables and recursion. Local functions are also considered to be more efficient than lambdas because they do not require the allocation of a delegate.

It is worth noting that when you write a lambda in VS Code, the editor will often suggest that you convert it to a local function, which hints at Microsoft's opinion on the matter:

```
    Console.WriteLine($"Converted text = { result}");
}                    Use local function (IDE0039)

                     (local variable) StringConverter converter
static void Main(str
{                    Quick Fix... (⌘.)
    StringConverter converter = s => s.ToLower();
```

Figure 16-1

16.10 Take the knowledge test

Click the link below or scan the QR code to test your knowledge and understanding of C# local functions and lambdas:

https://www.answertopia.com/v233

16.11 Summary

This chapter explored how anonymous methods, lambdas, and local functions enable you to write concise and reusable C# code that can be passed between methods. Lambdas result in more concise code than anonymous methods, while local functions have the advantage of conciseness, direct access to local variables, and support for recursion. Local functions are generally preferred over anonymous methods and lambdas for efficiency and local variable access.

Chapter 17

17. C# Inheritance

In *"An Introduction to C# Object-Oriented Programming"* we covered the basic concepts of object-oriented programming and worked through an example of creating and working with a new class using C#. In that example, our new class was not explicitly derived from a base class (though all C# classes are ultimately derived from the System.Object). This chapter will delve into the concepts of inheritance and subclassing in C#.

17.1 What is inheritance?

The concept of inheritance brings a real-world perspective to programming. It allows a class to be defined with a number of characteristics and then other classes to be derived from that class. The derived class inherits all of the features of the parent class and typically adds some of its own.

By deriving classes, we create what is often referred to as a *class hierarchy*. The class at the top of the hierarchy is known as the base class, and the derived classes are called subclasses. Any number of classes may be derived from a class. However, a derived class can only inherit from one class. As such, C# is known as a *single inheritance* programming language. Classes need not only be derived from a base class. For example, a subclass can also be inherited from another subclass.

17.2 A C# inheritance example

As with most programming concepts, the subject of inheritance in C# is best illustrated with an example. In the *"An Introduction to C# Object-Oriented Programming"* chapter, we created a project called ObjectDemo containing a BankAccount class. We will use this example to demonstrate C# inheritance.

Launch VS Code, open your "C# Essentials" workspace folder and use the Explorer panel to locate the *BankAccount.cs* file within the ObjectDemo project, as shown in Figure 17-1 below:

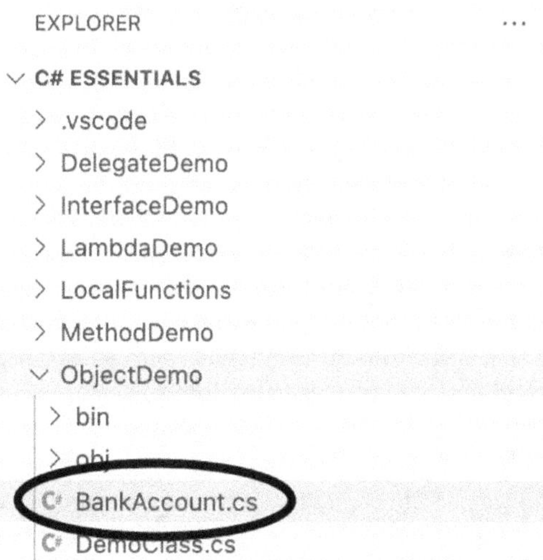

Figure 17-1

Once the project has loaded into VS Code, edit the *BankAccount.cs* file and add an additional field and property to the class to store the account balance:

```
namespace ObjectDemo;

public class BankAccount
{
    private string _accountName;
    private int _accountNumber;
    private double _accountBalance;

    public BankAccount(string accountName, int accountNumber,
                                                double accountBalance)
    {
        _accountName = accountName;
        _accountNumber = accountNumber;
        _accountBalance = accountBalance;
    }
.
.
    public double AccountBalance
    {
        get => _accountBalance;
        set => _accountBalance = value;
    }

    public void DisplayName()
    {
        Console.WriteLine($"Customer name is {AccountName}");
    }
.
.
}
```

This class does an excellent job of defining characteristics common to any type of bank account, such as account holder name, account number, and current balance. Imagine, however, that our banking program needs to support several specific types of bank accounts. For example, the bank might offer its customers an interest-bearing savings account. A savings account will have all the characteristics of our BankAccount class but would also need a way to store the prevailing interest rate. One option would be to create a brand new class from the ground up called SavingsAccount, which duplicates everything we have in our BankAccount class, plus extra members needed for a savings account. An alternative and more efficient method is to derive a SavingsAccount class from the BankAccount class and then add the extra functionality into this subclass.

17.3 Creating a subclass in C#

Now that we have ascertained that we need to create a subclass of our BankAccount class, we can look at how to achieve this. Subclasses are declared the same way as any other class, except that the class name is followed by a colon (:) and the name of the class from which it is to inherit.

With this in mind we can begin by using the Solution Explorer to add a new Class file to the project.

Using the Solution Explorer, hover the mouse pointer over the ObjectDemo project entry and click the new file button. In the file template palette, select the Class entry and name the new class SavingsAccount before pressing the Enter key to create the file. When the new file loads into the editor, modify the class declaration to subclass from BankAccount:

```
namespace ObjectDemo;

public class SavingsAccount : BankAccount
{

}
```

We have now created a subclass of BankAccount called SavingsAccount, but at this point, the SavingsAccount class is no different than its parent class. Next, we need to add a constructor and some new members to add the behavior we need:

```
public class SavingsAccount : BankAccount
{
    private double _interestRate;

    public SavingsAccount(string accountName, int accountNumber,
               double accountBalance, double interestRate)
                        : base(accountName, accountNumber, accountBalance)
    {
        _interestRate = interestRate;
    }

    public double InterestRate
    {
        get => _interestRate;
        set => _interestRate = value;
    }

    public double MonthlyInterest()
    {
        return (_interestRate * AccountBalance) / 12;
    }
}
```

We now have a new class called SavingsAccount, which inherits all the members of the BankAccount class and adds some members of its own. In particular, we have added a new data member called InterestRate, which will store the interest rate paid on the account together with a new method to calculate the monthly interest.

17.4 Passing arguments to the base class constructor

Of particular significance is the constructor in the SavingsAccount declaration. In the BankAccount base class, we have a constructor that accepts account name, number, and balance parameters. In the SavingsAccount subclass, we must also accept the interest rate value. The *: base()* code instructs C# to handle the name, number, and balance parameters using the constructor from the base BankAccount class, leaving the interest rate for the SavingsAccount constructor:

```
public SavingsAccount(string accountName, int accountNumber,
```

```
                double accountBalance, double interestRate)
                            : base(accountName, accountNumber, accountBalance)
```

With our SavingsAccount subclass complete, we can use it in our project. Edit the *Program.cs* file and modify it as follows:

```
using ObjectDemo;

SavingsAccount account = new(accountName: "John Smith", accountNumber: 12312,
accountBalance: 1000.99, interestRate: 0.05);

Console.WriteLine($"Interest earned this month = { account.MonthlyInterest()}");

account.DisplayName();
```

When it runs, the app will display the following output in the console:

```
Interest earned this month = 4.17079166666667
Customer name is John Smith
```

17.5 Overriding inherited methods

When using inheritance, it is not unusual to find a method in the parent class that almost does what you need but requires modification to provide the precise functionality you require. One option in this scenario would be to ignore the inherited method and write a new method with an entirely new name. A better option is to override the inherited method and write a new version in the subclass.

Before proceeding with an example, three rules must be obeyed when overriding a method:

1. The overriding method in the subclass must take the same number and types of parameters as the overridden method in the parent class.
2. The new method must have the same return type as the parent method.
3. The method declaration in the base class must be declared using virtual, abstract, or override modifiers.

The topics of abstract and virtual class members will be covered in the next chapter.

In our BankAccount class, we have a method named DisplayName(), which displays the account holder's name. In our SavingsAccount subclass, we might also want to output the current interest rate assigned to the account. To achieve this, the first step is to declare the method in the BankAccount class as being virtual:

```
public class BankAccount
{
.
.
    virtual public void DisplayName()
    {
        Console.WriteLine($"Customer name is {AccountName}");
    }
.
.
}
```

Next, we declare a new version of the DisplayBalance() method in our SavingsAccount subclass, prefixed with the override modifier:

```
public class SavingsAccount : BankAccount
{
.
.
    public override void DisplayName()
    {
        Console.WriteLine($"Customer name is { AccountName }");
        Console.WriteLine($"Account is earning { InterestRate }% interest.");
    }
}
```

Now, when we call the DisplayName() method on an instance of the SavingsAccount class, we get information about the customer's interest rate:

```
Interest earned this month = 4.17079166666667
Customer name is John Smith
Account is earning 0.05% interest.
```

It is also possible to call the overridden method in the base class from within a subclass. For example, the DisplayName() method of the base class could be called to display the account holder's name before the interest rate is displayed, thereby eliminating further code duplication. Using dot notation, we can call the method on the base object as follows:

```
public override void DisplayName()
{
    base.DisplayName();
    Console.WriteLine($"Account is earning { InterestRate }% interest.");
}
```

17.6 Take the knowledge test

Click the link below or scan the QR code to test your knowledge and understanding of C# inheritance:

https://www.answertopia.com/mdqq

17.7 Summary

In C#, inheritance is a programming concept that allows new classes to be created from existing classes and extended to add new functionality. This means that when an existing class provides some, but not all, of the functionality required by a programmer, that class can be used as the basis for a new subclass. By doing so, the new subclass will inherit all the parent class's capabilities and can be extended further to add any missing functionality.

Chapter 18

18. C# Abstract Classes

In the preceding chapters, we have examined object-oriented programming in C# and the concept of class inheritance. This chapter will introduce abstract classes.

18.1 What is a C# abstract class?

In the examples we have looked at so far in this book, we have created classes that could be both instantiated as objects and used as a base class from which to derive classes. Often, a base class is not intended to be instantiated and is provided solely as an outline or template for subclasses. Such a class is known as an abstract class. An abstract class cannot be instantiated as an object and is only provided to derive subclasses.

18.2 Abstract members

A C# abstract class contains abstract members, which define what a subclass must contain. These abstract members declare that a member of a particular type is required; it does not implement the member. Implementation of abstract members takes place within the derived class. A subclass that derives from an abstract class and fails to implement abstract methods will generate syntax errors.

18.3 Declaring a C# abstract class

In addition to using the class modifier, as we have seen in previous examples, abstract classes must also be declared using the abstract modifier:

```
public abstract class Talk {
}
```

Abstract class member methods and properties are also declared using the abstract keyword. For example, to declare an abstract method in our Talk class, the following code is required:

```
public abstract class Talk {
     public abstract void Speak();
}
```

We now have an abstract class with an abstract method named Speak(). Note that this declaration only states that any class derived from the Talk base class must implement a method called Speak() which returns no value (i.e., it is declared as void) and has no parameters. It does not, however, implement the method.

18.4 Deriving from an abstract class

To subclass from an abstract class, we write code as follows:

```
public class SayHello : Talk {
}
```

We now have a class named SayHello , which is derived from the abstract Talk class. The next step is to implement the abstract Speak() method. When implementing abstract members in a derived class, the override modifier must be used. For example:

```
public override void Speak() {
    Console.WriteLine("Hello!");
}
```

We now have a subclass derived from the Talk abstract class, which implements the abstract Speak() method.

18.5 Creating the AbstractClassDemo project

With the basics of abstract classes covered, we can put this knowledge to use in an example project. Begin by creating a new .NET Console App project in VS Code named AbstractClassDemo.

Using the Solution Explorer, add a new Class to the AbstractClassDemo project named *Talk*.

Edit the *Talk.cs* file to declare the Talk class as abstract and to add the abstract Speak() method as follows:

```
namespace AbstractClassDemo;

public abstract class Talk
{
    public abstract void Speak();
}
```

Next, we need to add the second class which will be subclassed from the Talk class. Repeat the above steps to add a class file to the project, this time naming the file *SayHello.cs*. Once the file has been added, make the following changes to subclass from Talk and implement the Speak() method:

```
namespace AbstractClassDemo
{
    internal class SayHello : Talk
    {
        public override void Speak()
        {
            Console.WriteLine("Hello!");
        }
    }
}
```

Finally, modify the *Program.cs* file to use the new classes:

```
using AbstractClassDemo;

SayHello demo = new();

demo.Speak();
```

Run the app to confirm that the "Hello!" message is displayed in the console.

18.6 Abstract vs. virtual members

So far, we have only looked at abstract class members. As discussed above, an abstract member is not implemented in the base class and must be implemented in derived classes for the class to compile.

Another type of member is a virtual member. A member defined as virtual must be implemented in the base class but may optionally be overridden in the derived class if different behavior is required. Virtual members are declared using the *virtual* modifier in the base class.

For example, modify the Talk class to include a virtual member named Goodbye() as follows:

```
namespace AbstractClassDemo;
```

```
public abstract class Talk
{
    public abstract void Speak();

    public virtual void Goodbye()
    {
        Console.WriteLine("Talk class says goodbye!");
    }
}
```

Next, make the following change in the *Program.cs* file to call the Goodbye() method:

```
SayHello demo = new();

demo.Speak();
demo.Goodbye();
```

When the app runs, output will be generated by both the Speak() and Goodbye() methods as follows:

```
Hello!
Talk class says goodbye!
```

Suppose we decide that the default Goodbye() method provided by the Talk class is not suitable for the requirements of the SayHello subclass. In that case, we can implement our own version of the method using the override modifier:

```
public class SayHello : Talk
{
    public override void Speak()
    {
        Console.WriteLine("Hello!");
    }

    public override void Goodbye()
    {
        Console.WriteLine("SayHello class says goodbye!");
    }
}
```

When the code executes, the Goodbye() method in the subclass is called instead of the virtual version in the Talk class:

```
Hello!
SayHello class says goodbye!
```

As with non-abstract classes, a subclass may call the base class implementation of a virtual method. For example, the subclass version of the Goodbye() method could be modified to also call the overridden base class Goodbye() method as follows:

```
public class SayHello : Talk
{
    public override void Speak()
```

```
    {
        Console.WriteLine("Hello!");
    }

    public override void Goodbye()
    {
        base.Goodbye();
        Console.WriteLine("SayHello class says goodbye!");
    }
}
```

When the Goodbye() method is called output from both variations will be displayed:

```
Hello!
Talk class says goodbye!
SayHello class says goodbye!
```

18.7 Take the knowledge test

Click the link below or scan the QR code to test your knowledge and understanding of C# abstract classes:

https://www.answertopia.com/76b9

18.8 Summary

Abstract classes are base classes that cannot be directly instantiated as objects. Instead, they provide a template that defines the requirements that subclasses must meet. The members of an abstract class can be declared abstract or virtual. Abstract members do not contain any implementation in the abstract class and must be overridden and implemented in derived classes. On the other hand, virtual members provide a fallback implementation within the abstract class to be used when the member is not overridden in subclasses.

Chapter 19

19. C# Interfaces

In this chapter, we will explain C# interfaces, how to write your own, and how to make other classes comply with one.

19.1 Understanding C# interfaces

By default, there are no specific rules to which a C# class must conform as long as the class is syntactically correct. In some situations, however, a class must meet specific criteria to work with other classes. This is particularly common when writing classes that need to work with other libraries. An interface is a set of rules that define the minimum requirements that a class must meet. An interface is declared using the *interface* keyword and defines the methods and properties that a class must contain to be in conformance. When a class adopts an interface but does not meet all the interface requirements, errors will be reported stating that the class fails to conform to the interface. Unlike abstract classes, an interface does not contain implementations of members.

19.2 Declaring an interface

Interfaces are declared much like other classes except that we use *interface* keyword instead of *class* in the declaration. Consider the following interface declaration. Any classes that adopt this interface must include a method named DemoMethod(), which accepts no parameters and returns a string value:

```
interface IDemoInterface
{
    void DemoMethod();
}
```

Note that the convention is to prefix interface names with "I" to differentiate them from non-interface classes.

Unlike abstract classes, an interface must not contain implementations of its members. The following, for example, is not a valid interface:

```
interface IDemoInterface
{
    void DemoMethod()
    {
        Console.WriteLine("Hello");
    }
}
```

The above code will generate the following syntax error:

```
Error  CS8701 Target runtime doesn't support default interface implementation.
```

To comply with the IDemoInterface interface, a class must include a DemoMethod() implementation matching the interface method signature. For example:

```
public class DemoClass : IDemoInterface
{
    public void DemoMethod()
    {
```

```
        // Code here
    }
}
```

19.3 Creating the InterfaceDemo project

With the basics of C# interfaces covered, we can put this knowledge to use in an example project. Begin by creating a new .NET Console App project in VS Code named InterfaceDemo.

19.4 Adding a C# interface file

The next step is to use the Solution Explorer to add a new interface file to our project. The Solution Explorer is located at the bottom of the Explorer panel as shown in Figure 19-1:

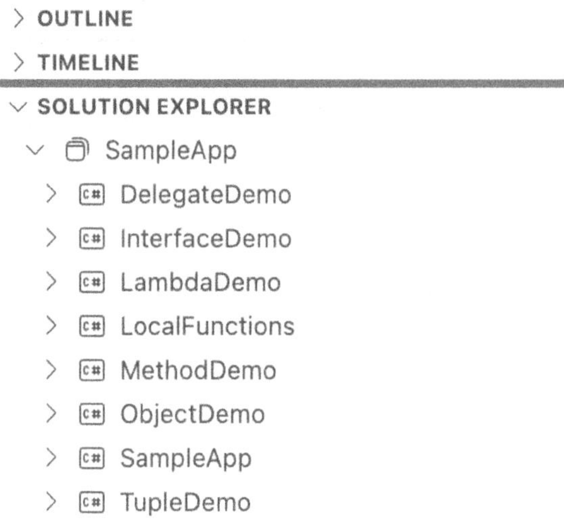

Figure 19-1

Within the Solution Explorer, hover the mouse pointer over the InterfaceDemo entry to display the new file and folder buttons:

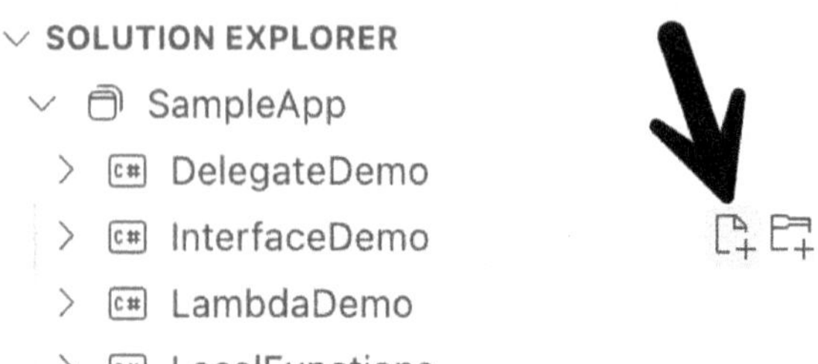

Figure 19-2

Click the new file button indicated by the arrow in Figure 19-2 above to display the Add New File palette as shown in Figure 19-3. Within the palette, select the Interface option:

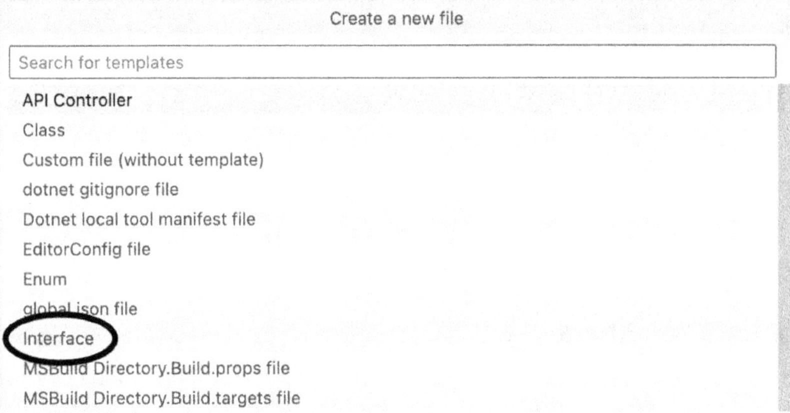

Figure 19-3

When prompted, name the interface *IMessageBuilder* before pressing Enter to create the file. The new file will automatically load into the editor, where it will read as follows:

```
namespace InterfaceDemo;

public interface IMessageBuilder
{

}
```

Modify the interface declaration to add an interface member named ShowMessage():

```
namespace InterfaceDemo;

public interface IMessageBuilder
{
    void ShowMessage();
}
```

Any class that adopts the IMessageBuilder interface must include a ShowMessage() member. Use the Solutions Explorer to add a Class file to the project named MyMessageBuilder and modify it to implement the IMessageBuilder interface as follows:

```
namespace InterfaceDemo;

public class MyMessageBuilder : IMessageBuilder
{

}
```

After the above change has been made, the editor will report the following error:

```
'MyMessageBuilder' does not implement interface member 'IMessageBuilder.
ShowMessage()'
```

The MyMessageBuilder class generates this error because it does not contain an implementation of the ShowMessage() method as required by the IMessageBuilder interface. To conform to the interface, we need to implement the ShowMessage() method:

```
namespace InterfaceDemo;

public class MyMessageBuilder : IMessageBuilder
{
    public void ShowMessage()
    {

    }
}
```

19.5 Interface data members

Interfaces can include data members in addition to methods. An important rule when working with interfaces is that variables must be declared as properties and cannot be declared as fields or constants (for a reminder of the differences between fields and properties, refer back to the *"An Introduction to C# Object-Oriented Programming"* chapter). The following declaration, therefore, will generate a syntax error:

```
public interface IMessageBuilder
{
    string myMessage; // Fields are invalid in interfaces
    void ShowMessage();
}
```

Instead, the variable needs to be declared as a property:

```
public interface IMessageBuilder
{
    string MyMessage { get; set; }
    void ShowMessage();
}
```

Note that get and set accessor methods are declared but not implemented in the above interface. As interface methods, the implementation is performed in the conforming class declaration.

Now that the IMessageBuilder interface requires a string property named MyMessage, we need to modify the MyMessageBuilder class accordingly:

```
public class MyMessageBuilder : IMessageBuilder
{
    private string _myMessage = "";

    public string MyMessage
    {
        get => _myMessage;
        set => _myMessage = value;
    }

    public void ShowMessage()
    {
        Console.WriteLine(_myMessage);
    }
```

```
}
```

Next, modify the *Program.cs* file to create the MyMessageBuilder object and call the ShowMessage() method:

```
using InterfaceDemo;

MyMessageBuilder msgBuilder = new()
{
    MyMessage = "Interface Demo"
};

msgBuilder.ShowMessage();
```

Finally, build and run the app to test that the message is displayed.

19.6 Take the knowledge test

Click the link below or scan the QR code to test your knowledge and understanding of C# Interfaces:

https://www.answertopia.com/2tw1

19.7 Summary

C# interfaces define minimum requirements for classes, ensuring compatibility with other libraries. To conform with an interface, classes must implement matching interface methods and properties. Interfaces can include data members, which must be declared as properties.

Chapter 20

20. C# Structures

Having covered C# classes in the preceding chapters, this chapter will introduce the use of structures in C#. Although at first glance structures and classes look similar, there are some important differences that need to be understood when deciding which to use. This chapter will outline how to declare and use structures, explore the differences between structures and classes and introduce the concepts of value and reference types.

20.1 An overview of C# structures

As with classes, structures form the basis of object-oriented programming and provide a way to encapsulate data and functionality into reusable instances. Structure declarations resemble classes with the exception that the struct keyword is used in place of the class keyword. The following code, for example, declares a simple structure consisting of a String variable, initializer, and method:

```
public struct SampleStruct(string name)
{
    private string _name = name;

    public string Name {
        get => _name;
        set => _name = value;
    }

    public string BuildHelloMsg() {
        return "Hello " + _name;
    }
}
```

Consider the above structure declaration in comparison to the equivalent class declaration:

```
public class SampleClass(string name)
{
    private string _name = name;

    public string Name {
        get => _name;
        set => _name = value;
    }

    public string BuildHelloMsg() {
        return "Hello " + _name;
    }
}
```

Other than the use of the struct keyword instead of class, the two declarations are identical. Instances of each type are also created using the same syntax:

```
SampleStruct demoStruct = new(name: "Alex");
SampleClass demoClass = new(name: "Anna");
```

Given the commonality between classes and structures, it is important to gain an understanding of how the two differ. Before exploring the most significant difference it is first necessary to understand the concepts of value types and reference types.

20.2 Creating the StructureDemo project

Launch VS Code, open your "C# Essentials" workspace folder and create a new .NET Console App project named StructureDemo.

20.3 Value types vs. reference types

While on the surface structures and classes look alike, major differences in behavior occur when structure and class instances are copied or passed as arguments to methods. This occurs because structure instances are *value type* while class instances are *reference type.*

When a structure instance is copied or passed to a method, an actual copy of the instance is created, together with any data contained within the instance. This means that the copy has its own version of the data which is unconnected with the original structure instance. In effect, this means that there can be multiple copies of a structure instance within a running app, each with its own local copy of the associated data. A change to one instance has no impact on any other instances.

In contrast, when a class instance is copied or passed as an argument, the only thing duplicated or passed is a reference to the location in memory where that class instance resides. Any changes made to the instance using those references will be performed on the same instance. In other words, there is only one class instance but multiple references pointing to it. A change to the instance data using any one of those references changes the data for all other references.

20.4 Adding the Struct declaration

To demonstrate reference and value types in action, use the Solution Explorer to add a new Struct named SampleStruct to the StructureDemo project. Follow the usual steps to add the file, this time selecting the Strut option from the file template panel as highlighted in Figure 20-1:

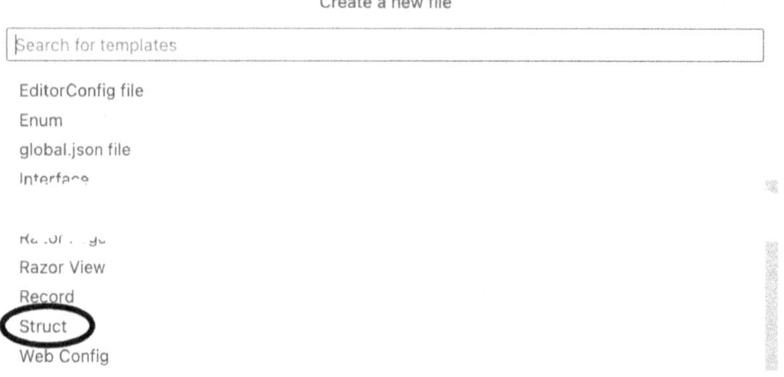

Figure 20-1

Once the file has been created, modify it to read as follows:

```
namespace StructureDemo;

public struct SampleStruct(string name)
```

```
{
    private string _name = name;

    public string Name {
        get => _name;
        set => _name = value;
    }

    public string BuildHelloMsg() {
        return "Hello " + _name;
    }
}
```

Next, edit the *Program.cs* file to create a SampleStruct instance and call the BuildHelloMsg() method:

```
using StructureDemo;

SampleStruct myStruct1 = new(name: "Mark");
Console.WriteLine(myStruct1.BuildHelloMsg());
```

When the code executes, the message "Hello Mark" will be displayed. Now change the code so that a copy of the myStruct1 instance is made, the name property is changed, and the names from each instance are displayed in the message:

```
SampleStruct myStruct1 = new(name: "Mark");
SampleStruct myStruct2 = myStruct1;
myStruct2.Name = "David";

Console.WriteLine(myStruct1.BuildHelloMsg());
Console.WriteLine(myStruct2.BuildHelloMsg());
```

When executed, the output will read as follows:

```
Hello Mark
Hello David
```

Clearly, the change of name only applied to myStruct2 since this is an actual copy of myStruct1 containing its own copy of the data as shown in the following figure:

Figure 20-2

To contrast this behavior with an equivalent class, add a Class named SampleClass to the project, and implement it as follows:

```
namespace StructureDemo;
```

```
public class SampleClass(string name)
{
    private string _name = name;

    public string Name {
        get => _name;
        set => _name = value;
    }

    public string BuildHelloMsg() {
        return "Hello " + _name;
    }
}
```

With the class added to the project, modify the *Program.cs* file to repeat the operations performed in the structure example:

```
SampleClass myClass1 = new(name: "Mark");
SampleClass myClass2 = myClass1;
myClass2.Name = "David";

Console.WriteLine(myClass1.BuildHelloMsg());
Console.WriteLine(myClass2.BuildHelloMsg());
```

When this code executes, the following output will be generated:

```
Hello David
Hello David
```

In this case, the name property change is reflected for both myClass1 and myClass2 because both are references pointing to the same class instance as illustrated in the figure below:

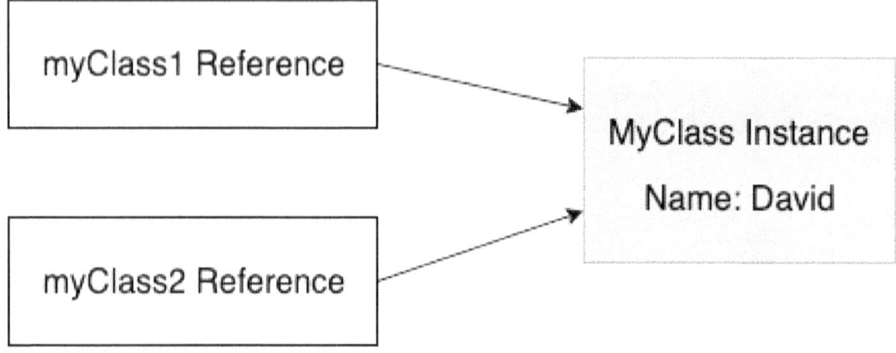

Figure 20-3

In addition to these value and reference type differences, structures do not support inheritance and subclassing in the way that classes do. In other words, it is not possible for one structure to inherit from another structure. Unlike classes, structures also cannot contain a finalizer method. Structure members cannot be specified as abstract, virtual, or protected. Structures can, however, implement interfaces.

20.5 Read-only structures

Structures can be declared as being read-only using the *readonly* modifier. When declared in this way, all data members of the structure must also be declared as being read-only. In the case of field members, this requires the use of the *readonly* modifier. Properties, on the other hand, must either be declared as *readonly* or use the *init-only* accessors (a topic covered in the chapter entitled *"An Introduction to C# Object-Oriented Programming"*).

The following structure, for example, includes both a read-only field and an init-only property:

```
namespace StructureDemo;

public readonly struct SampleStruct(string name)
{
    private readonly string _name = name;

    public string Name {
        get => _name;
    }

    public string BuildHelloMsg() {
        return "Hello " + _name;
    }
}
```

20.6 Take the knowledge test

Click the link below or scan the QR code to test your knowledge and understanding of C# structures:

https://www.answertopia.com/i5tf

20.7 Summary

C# structures and classes provide a mechanism for creating instances that define properties, store values, and define methods. Although the two mechanisms appear similar, significant behavioral differences exist, especially when structure and class instances are copied or passed to a method. Classes are categorized as reference-type instances, while structures are value-type. When a structure instance is copied or passed, an entirely new copy of the instance is created containing its own data. On the other hand, class instances are passed and copied by reference, with each reference pointing to the same class instance. Other features unique to classes include support for inheritance and finalizers.

Chapter 21

21. C# Tuple Type

In the *"C# Methods"* chapter, we learned how to create methods in C# that can pass arguments and return results. This chapter will focus on the C# tuple type and understand how it combines collections of values into a single entity. Once created, a tuple can be passed from one method to another while allowing methods to return multiple results in a single return value. Tuples can be created with minimal coding and can store data of any type. Additionally, the values stored within a tuple are not required to be the same type.

21.1 Creating the TupleDemo project

To try out the C# tuple type, launch VS Code, open your "C# Essentials" workspace folder and create a new .NET Console App project named TupleDemo.

21.2 Declaring a Tuple

When we declare a tuple we need to provide it with the values to be stored and, optionally, the corresponding value types. The syntax for declaring a tuple is as follows:

```
(<type1>, <type2>, ...) <tuplename> = (<value1>, <value2>, ...)
```

For example, modify the *Program.cs* file as follows, to add the top-level statements, the Main() method, and a method named GetProductData() that contains a tuple declaration:

```
namespace TupleDemo
{
    internal class Program
    {
        static void Main(string[] args)
        {
            GetProductData();
        }

        private static void GetProductData()
        {
            (int, string, double) myTuple = (10, "Refrigerator", 432.43);
        }
    }
}
```

If you prefer not to declare the type of each tuple value, the var keyword may be used to tell the compiler to infer the value types:

```
var myTuple = (10,  "Refrigerator", 432.43);
```

21.3 Accessing tuple values

The elements of a tuple can be accessed using several different techniques. A specific tuple value may be accessed using dot notation to access Item<n> where <n> is the number of the item (with the first value being at position 1). The code below, for example, extracts item 2 from the tuple, assigns it to a variable and writes it to the console:

```
private static void GetProductData()
```

```
{
    var myTuple = (10, "Refrigerator", 432.43);
    var item2 = myTuple.Item2;

    Console.WriteLine(item2);
}
```

An alternative to accessing tuple elements by item number is to use field names.

21.4 Tuple field names

When creating a tuple, you can assign a name to each value. The names assigned to the values stored in a tuple can then be used when you reference those values in code, for example:

```
(int Count, string Product, double Price) myTuple = (10, "Refrigerator", 432.43);
```

When using type inference to initialize a tuple, the field names are placed before each value:

```
var myTuple = (Count: 10, Product: "Refrigerator", Price: 432.43);
```

Once field names have been assigned, the corresponding values are accessed using dot notation, as demonstrated in the code changes below:

```
private static void GetProductData()
{
    var myTuple = (Count: 10, Product: "Refrigerator", Price: 432.43);

    Console.WriteLine($"myTuple Price = { myTuple.Price}");
    Console.WriteLine($"myTuple Product = { myTuple.Product}");
    Console.WriteLine($"myTuple Quantity = { myTuple.Count}");
}
```

The following output will appear in the console when the app runs:

```
myTuple Price = 432.43
myTuple Product = Refrigerator
myTuple Quantity = 10
```

21.5 Returning tuples from methods

Tuples are particularly useful for returning multiple results from a method. For example, suppose that instead of displaying product information, we need our GetProductData() method to return the data. To achieve this, the type of each tuple value needs to be included in the method return type declaration as follows:

```
private static (int, string, double) GetProductData()
{
.
.
}
```

When returning the tuple from within the method, we can return an existing tuple as follows:

```
private static (int, string, double) GetProductData()
{
    var myTuple = (Count: 10, Product: "Refrigerator", Price: 432.43);

    return myTuple;
```

```
}
```

Alternatively, the individual values can be returned by placing them in parentheses after the return statement:

```
private static (int, string, double) GetProductData()
{
    return (10, "Refrigerator", 432.43);
}
```

When called, the returned tuple can be assigned to a variable, and the individual values accessed using dot notation:

```
static void Main(string[] args)
{
    var myTuple = GetProductData();

    Console.WriteLine($"myTuple Price = {myTuple.Item1}");
    Console.WriteLine($"myTuple Product = {myTuple.Item2}");
    Console.WriteLine($"myTuple Quantity = {myTuple.Item3}");
}
```

If you prefer to use field names instead of the Item<n> default names, one option is to include the field names and types as follows:

```
static void Main(string[] args)
{
    (int Count, string Product, double Price) myTuple = GetProductData();

    Console.WriteLine($"myTuple Price = {myTuple.Price}");
    Console.WriteLine($"myTuple Product = {myTuple.Product}");
    Console.WriteLine($"myTuple Quantity = {myTuple.Count}");
}
```

By far, the most convenient way to assign each tuple value to a named variable is to use type inference. The following code, for example, assigns the three values in the tuple returned by GetProductData() to variables named *count*, *product*, and *price*:

```
var (count, product, price) = GetProductData();
```

Using this approach, we can now access the variables directly without needing first to extract them from the tuple:

```
static void Main(string[] args)
{
    var (count, product, price) = GetProductData();

    Console.WriteLine($"Price = {price}");
    Console.WriteLine($"Product = {product}");
    Console.WriteLine($"Quantity = {count}");
}
```

21.6 Tuples as method parameters

In addition to returning tuple results from methods, you can also pass tuples to methods. A method designed to accept our example tuple as an argument could be declared as follows:

```
public static void DisplayProductData((int, string, double) productTuple)
{
}
```

Alternatively, the tuple values may be assigned field names:

```
public static void DisplayProductData((int count, string description,
                                      double price) productTuple)
{
}
```

Once the method is declared, we can pass it a tuple in several ways. One option is to pass through the literal value to the method:

```
DisplayProductData((20, "Water filter", 29.99));
```

Another option is, of course, to create a tuple object and pass it to the method:

```
var myTuple = (20, "Water filter", 29.99);

DisplayProductData(myTuple);
```

Modify the *Program.cs* file to add the DisplayProductData() method and to pass it a tuple argument:

```
static void Main(string[] args)
{
    var myTuple = GetProductData();

    DisplayProductData(myTuple);
}

public static void DisplayProductData((int, string, double) productTuple)
{
    var (count, product, price) = productTuple;

    Console.WriteLine($"Price = {price}");
    Console.WriteLine($"Product = {product}");
    Console.WriteLine($"Quantity = {count}");
}
```

Run the app and verify that the product information is displayed in the console.

21.7 Take the knowledge test

Click the link below or scan the QR code to test your knowledge and understanding of the C# Tuple type:

https://www.answertopia.com/pxci

21.8 Summary

C# tuples allow us to temporarily group multiple values into a single entity. Once declared, a tuple can be used to return groups of result values from a method or to pass multiple parameter values between methods within a single argument. Tuples support most C# data types, including custom objects, and their items do not have to be of matching types. We can access tuple items by item number and field name or assign them directly to named variables.

Chapter 22

22. C# Namespaces

In the preceding chapters, we have covered object-oriented C# programming in detail. We have learned how code is structured using classes and structures that result in well-organized re-usable code. In many of the code examples used so far, we have seen namespace declarations. Now that we understand object-oriented programming, we are ready to find out what namespaces are, why they exist, and how to use them.

22.1 Understanding scope

Before we talk about namespaces, we first need to understand the concept of *scope* as it relates to programming languages. Scope defines whether entities such as class declarations, methods, and variables are visible and accessible to code that resides outside the current scope. We touched on scope briefly when looking at C# looping. For example, variables declared within a body of a *for* loop belong only to the loop's scope and do not exist before or after the loop executes:

```
// variable myCounter does not yet exist


for (int i = 0; i < 10; i++)
{
        int myCounter = 0; //myCounter variable created in scope of for loop
        myCounter += i;
}

// after loop exit variable myCounter is now out of scope and ceases to exist
```

Similarly, class methods and properties reside in the scope of the class in which they are declared and can only be accessed by referencing the containing class. In the following example, we can only access the IncrementCounter() method by referencing MyClass:

```
class MyClass
{
    static int myCountr = 0;

    public static void IncrementCounter() {
        myCounter++;
    }
}

MyClass.IncrementCounter();
```

Scope allows us to declare classes and structures without worrying that a method name in one class might conflict with a method in another class. For example, the identical method names in the following classes do not conflict because they belong to separate scopes:

```
class MyClass
{
    static int myCounter = 0;
```

```
    public static void IncrementCounter() {
        myCounter++;
    }
}

class MyOtherClass
{
    static int myCounter = 0;

    public static void IncrementCounter() {
        myCounter++;
    }
}
```

A problem arises, however, when entities like classes and structures themselves have conflicting names. If both of the above classes were named MyClass, the code would generate a syntax error because they are declared within the same scope. The solution to this is to use namespaces.

22.2 An overview of namespaces

Much like classes and structures, namespaces provide an additional layer of organization within C# code. As we have seen, a C# project contains classes and structures containing members, spread across multiple source code files.

Particularly within large projects with complex code bases, there is a possibility that names that are not declared within the scope of class or structure will conflict with each other, either in the code you have written or between your code and the built-in .NET classes and structures. The following code, for example, will trigger a syntax error because the class names conflict:

```
class ClassA
{
    public static void OpenFile() {
        Console.WriteLine("Class A OpenFile()");
    }
}

class ClassA
{
    public static void OpenFile()
    {
        Console.WriteLine("Class A OpenFile()");
    }
}
```

Namespaces allow application code to be organized into separate scopes (called *spaces*) so that the names in one namespace do not conflict with the same names in another. In the absence of a specific namespace, declarations such as those above are members of the *global namespace*, as illustrated in Figure 22-1 below:

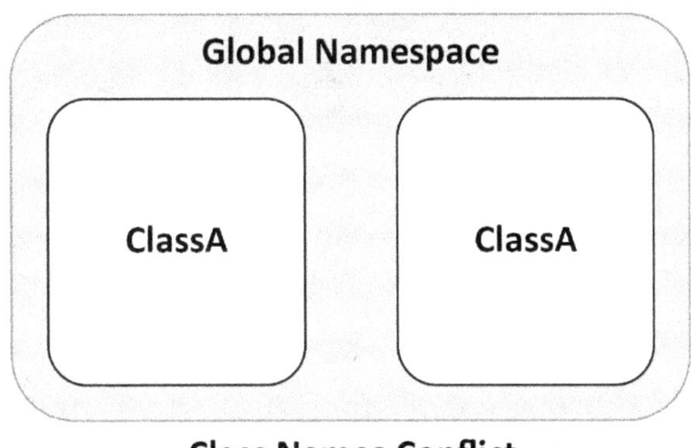

Figure 22-1

Aside from renaming one of the classes, the only way to resolve the ClassA naming conflict is to move one or both classes into separate namespaces. In the rest of this chapter, we will create a project to resolve the above problem and explore namespaces in more detail.

22.3 Creating the NamespaceDemo project

Launch VS Code, open your "C# Essentials" workspace folder, and create a new .NET Console App project named NamespaceDemo.

Locate the new project in the Explorer panel, edit the *Program.cs* file, and replace the existing code with the following:

```
class ClassA {
    public static void OpenFile() {
        Console.WriteLine("First ClassA OpenFile()");
    }
}

class ClassA {
    public static void OpenFile() {
        Console.WriteLine("Second ClassA OpenFile()");
    }
}

namespace SampleApp
{
    internal class Program
    {
        static void Main(string[] args)
        {
        }
    }
}
```

At this point, the editor will report the following syntax error in the second ClassA declaration

```
The namespace '<global namespace>' already contains a definition for 'ClassA'
```

This tells us that both classes reside in the same namespace (in this case the global namespace) and have conflicting names. To resolve this we need to create another namespace.

22.4 Declaring namespaces

Namespaces are declared using the *namespace* keyword followed by a name and braces encapsulating the namespace members. To resolve the naming conflict, we can place the second ClassA declaration into a separate namespace, leaving the first in the global namespace:

```
class ClassA {
    public static void OpenFile()
    {
        Console.WriteLine("ClassA OpenFile()");
    }
}

namespace DemoSpace
{
   class ClassA {
       public static void OpenFile()
       {
           Console.WriteLine("Second ClassA OpenFile()");
       }
   }
}
.
.
```

After making the above changes, the duplicate definition error should be resolved:

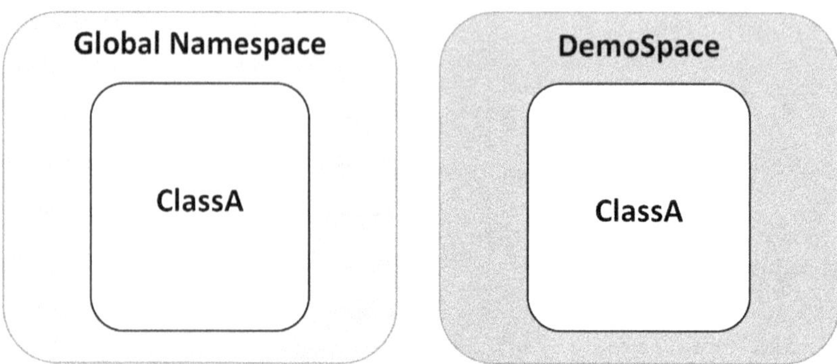

Figure 22-2

A single source file can contain multiple namespaces. Modify the example to include two namespaces as follows:

```
namespace DemoSpaceOne
{
    class ClassA
```

```
    {
        public static void OpenFile()
        {
            Console.WriteLine("First ClassA OpenFile()");
        }
    }
}

namespace DemoSpaceTwo
{
    class ClassA
    {
        public static void OpenFile()
        {
            Console.WriteLine("Second ClassA OpenFile()");
        }
    }
}
```

With this change, our project now contains three namespaces (in addition to the System namespace required for the Console WriteLine() calls): DemoSpaceOne, DemoSpaceTwo, and the global namespace:

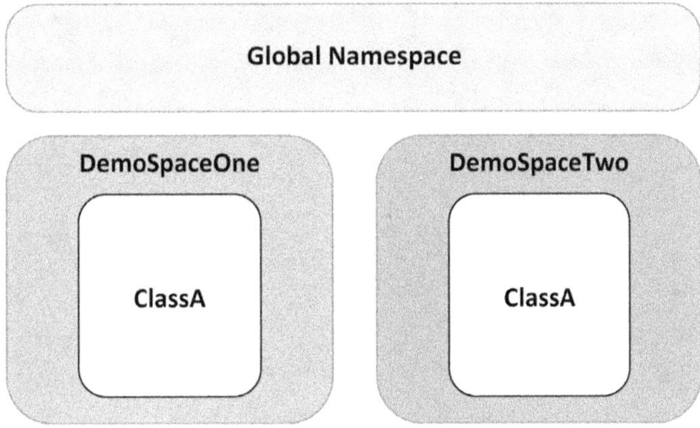

Figure 22-3

22.5 Accessing namespace members

With the two ClassA definitions contained within separate namespaces, we need a way to tell the compiler which class we are accessing. Using dot notation, we can differentiate the classes by referencing the corresponding namespace. Modify the Main() method as follows to call the OpenFile() method belonging to each ClassA implementation:

```
namespace SampleApp
{
    internal class Program
    {
        static void Main(string[] args)
```

```
        {
            DemoSpaceOne.ClassA.OpenFile();
            DemoSpaceTwo.ClassA.OpenFile();
        }
    }
}
```

Compile and run the app and verify that the output listed below appears in the Terminal:

```
First ClassA OpenFile()
Second ClassA OpenFile()
```

22.6 Namespaces and the "using" keyword

An alternative to dot notation is the *using* keyword which tells the compiler which namespace to use by default in the absence of an explicit namespace declaration. For example, the following changes will default to DemoSpaceTwo when no namespace is specified in the Main() method:

```
using DemoSpaceTwo;

namespace DemoSpaceOne
{
.
.
}

namespace DemoSpaceTwo
{
.
.
}

namespace SampleApp
{
    internal class Program
    {
        static void Main(string[] args)
        {
            ClassA.OpenFile();
        }
    }
}
```

When the app runs, the ClassA.OpenFile() method belonging to the DemoSpaceTwo namespace will be called:

```
Second ClassA OpenFile()
```

To access the DemoSpaceOne OpenFile() method, however, we must still override the default namespace specified by the *using* statement as follows:

```
using DemoSpaceTwo;
```

```
static void Main(string[] args)
{
    ClassA.OpenFile() // Defaults to DemoSpaceTwo
    DemoSpaceOne.ClassA.OpenFile(); // Explicitly selects DemoSpaceOne
}
```

22.7 Nested namespaces

Namespaces can be declared within other namespaces to create a nested hierarchy. To experience nested namespaces, add the following namespace declaration to the *Program.cs* file:

```
namespace DemoOne
{
    namespace DemoTwo
    {
        namespace DemoThree
        {
            class ClassC
            {
                public static string message = "DemoThree message";
            }
        }
    }
}
```

To access the message field we need to reference each of the containing namespaces:

```
static void Main(string[] args)
{
    var message = DemoOne.DemoTwo.DemoThree.ClassC.message;
    Console.WriteLine(message);
}
```

When the app runs, the output will now DemoThree message.

22.8 Aliases and the namespace alias operator

C# allows the *using* keyword to assign aliases to namespace references. Using this technique, we can assign an alias to our nested namespace as follows:

```
using DemoSpaceTwo;
using MyAlias = DemoOne.DemoTwo.DemoThree;
.
.
```

To access ClassC using the alias, we use the alias operator (::):

```
static void Main(string[] args)
{
    ClassA.OpenFile();
    DemoSpaceOne.ClassA.OpenFile();

    var message = MyAlias::ClassC.message;
```

```
    Console.WriteLine(message);
}
```

Note that the alias declaration has not overridden the "using DemoSpaceTwo" statement and we are still able to access the OpenFile() method from the second ClassA without referencing the namespace:

```
ClassA.OpenFile();
```

The alias operator can also be used to explicitly access objects in the global namespace. Consider the following code sample consisting of a class that is declared both in the global namespace and within a class in a custom namespace:

```
class MyString
{
    public static string text = "Global string";
}

namespace SampleApp
{
    class MyString
    {
        public static string text = "Local string";
    }

    internal class Program
    {
        static void Main(string[] args)
        {
            Console.WriteLine(MyString.text);
        }
    }
}
```

When the above code executes, the text from the local MyString class will be displayed. To access the global class, we can use the alias operator to specify the *global* namespace:

```
static void Main(string[] args)
{
    Console.WriteLine(MyString.text);
    Console.WriteLine(global::MyString.text);
}
```

22.9 File scoped namespaces

If the entire contents of a source file is to belong to the same namespace, a file scoped declaration can be used. In the following code, ClassA and ClassB are both declared within the FileScopeSpace namespace:

```
namespace FileScopeSpace;

class ClassA
{
    public static void OpenFile()
```

```
    {
        Console.WriteLine("Class A OpenFile()");
    }
}

class ClassB
{
    public static void OpenFile()
    {
       Console.WriteLine("Class B OpenFile()");
    }
}
```

File scoped namespaces cannot include other namespaces. The following, therefore, is invalid syntax:

```
namespace FileScopeSpace;

class ClassA
{
    public static void OpenFile()
    {
        Console.WriteLine("Class A OpenFile()");
    }
}

namespace SpaceOne // Invalid namespace declaration
{
     class ClassB
     {
        public static void OpenFile()
        {
           Console.WriteLine("Class B OpenFile()");
        }
    }
}
```

22.10 Take the knowledge test

Click the link below or scan the QR code to test your knowledge and understanding of C# namespaces:

https://www.answertopia.com/bkx3

22.11 Summary

In this chapter, we have explored C# namespaces and learned how they are used to organize project code and avoid naming conflicts. Namespaces are declared using the *namespace* keyword and accessed using dot notation. File-scoped namespaces allow entire source files to be designated as belonging to the same namespace.

Chapter 23

23. C# Exception Handling

In a perfect world, C# code would never encounter an error. Since we don't live in a perfect world, it's impossible to guarantee that an error (more commonly referred to as an *exception*) won't occur while your code is executing. Therefore, it's crucial to ensure the code gracefully handles any exceptions that may arise.

This chapter covers exception handling using C#, introducing topics like exception types, how exceptions are thrown, and how to handle them using *try-catch* statements.

23.1 Understanding exception handling

No matter how meticulously your C# code is designed and implemented, there will always be situations beyond the app's control. For instance, an app relying on an active network connection can't control the loss of that connection. What the app can do, however, is implement robust exception handling, like displaying a message to the user, or silently attempting to re-establish the lost network connection.

Exception handling in C# involves two main aspects: triggering (or throwing) an exception when desired results aren't achieved within a method and catching and handling the exception after it's thrown by another method.

When an exception is thrown, it has a specific exception type that can be used to identify the nature of the exception and decide on the most appropriate course of action. When throwing exceptions in your code, you can use the built-in exception types, or create and throw custom exception types derived from the System Exception class.

While learning about exception handling in C#, remember that in addition to implementing code in your app to throw exceptions when necessary, many API methods in the C# and .NET frameworks also throw exceptions that must be handled within your app's code. Failure to do so typically results in a runtime exception and your app crashing.

23.2 Creating the ExceptionDemo project

Launch VS Code, open your "C# Essentials" workspace folder, and create a new .NET Console App project named ExceptionDemo. Once the project is ready, modify the *Program.cs* file as follows:

```
namespace ExceptionDemo
{
    internal class Program
    {
        static void Main(string[] args)
        {


        }
    }
}
```

The project is a hypothetical app that controls an electric motor. During the power-on diagnostics, the app reads the current voltage and prevents the motor from starting if it exceeds 500 volts. Remaining in the *Program.cs* file, add a method to perform the voltage check and call it from the Main() method:

```
namespace ExceptionDemo
{
    internal class Program
    {
        static void Main(string[] args)
        {
            VoltageCheck(501);
        }

        private static void VoltageCheck(int voltage)
        {
            if (voltage > 500)
            {
                Console.WriteLine("Voltage overload.");
            }
            else
            {
                Console.WriteLine("Voltage is safe.");
            }
        }
    }
}
```

Run the app and check that the voltage overload message appears in the console:

```
Voltage overload.
```

A voltage overload is a serious issue, so we want to do more than display a message and hope the user doesn't just start the motor. Instead, we want to force the app to take preventative measures. To do this, we will throw an exception.

23.3 Throwing exceptions

The first step in throwing an exception is to choose an exception type. As we mentioned previously, exceptions can be thrown using one of the many built-in types or a custom type you have created. We will cover custom exception types later in the chapter, so for now, we will use the ArgumentOutOfRangeException type. This exception type is typically thrown when an argument passed to a method is outside an acceptable range (in our case a voltage reading exceeding 500 volts).

Next, an instance of the exception type is created and initialized. All exception types must be initialized with a message explaining the cause of the problem. Some types, including ArgumentOutOfRangeException, also require the name of the parameter that caused the exception (in our case, the voltage). With this information, we can create a new exception as follows:

```
ArgumentOutOfRangeException voltageException = new(nameof(voltage), "Voltage
exceeds safety parameters.");
```

Exceptions are thrown using the *throw* statement followed by the exception object, as follows:

```
throw voltageException;
```

In the above examples, we have created and thrown the exception as separate steps. This sequence is, however, typically performed in a single operation:

```
throw new ArgumentOutOfRangeException(nameof(voltage), "Voltage exceeds safety parameters.");
```

Modify the VoltageCheck() method to throw an exception as follows:

```
private static void VoltageCheck(int voltage)
{
    if (voltage > 500)
    {
        throw new ArgumentOutOfRangeException(nameof(voltage),
                                "Voltage exceeds safety parameters.");
    }
    else
    {
        Console.WriteLine("Safe Voltage");
    }
}
```

Refer to the console, where the following output will appear:

```
Unhandled exception. System.ArgumentOutOfRangeException: Voltage exceeds safety parameters. (Parameter 'voltage')
   at ExceptionDemo.Program.VoltageCheck(Int32 voltage) in Program.cs:line 16
   at ExceptionDemo.Program.Main(String[] args) in Program.cs:line 8
```

This message tells us the app was terminated due to an unhandled exception. The error includes the exception type, the message, and the name of the parameter that caused the exception.

We now need to add additional code to handle the exception when it is thrown.

23.4 Handling exceptions

Exceptions in C# are handled using *try-catch* statements. To prevent our app from crashing when the exception is thrown, we must make the following changes to the Main() method:

```
static void Main(string[] args)
{
    try
    {
        VoltageCheck(501);
    }
    catch
    {
        Console.WriteLine("Voltage too high - disconnecting power");
    }
}
```

When the app runs, the *try-catch* statement will handle the exception and allow the app to take corrective action.

It is also possible to access the exception object within the body of the catch block, providing access to the message:

```
try
{
```

```
    VoltageCheck(501);
}

catch (ArgumentOutOfRangeException ex)
{
    Console.WriteLine(ex.Message);
}
```

So far, we have implemented code to handle a single exception type. The code within the body of the try block may, however, throw a variety of exception types. By accessing the exception object, we can identify the exception type and take type-specific actions. For example:

```
catch (Exception ex)
{
    if (ex is ArgumentOutOfRangeException)
    {
        Console.WriteLine(ex.Message);
    }
    else if (ex is NullReferenceException)
    {
        Console.WriteLine(ex.Message);
    }
}
```

23.5 Creating exception filters with the "when" keyword

In the above example, we used an *if ... else if* statement to take different actions depending on the type of the caught exception. The *when* keyword provides a higher-level filtering option to control whether a catch block meets specific rules. The syntax for using *when* in a catch block is as follows:

```
try
{
}
catch (<exception>) when (<boolean expression>)
{

}
```

The code within the catch block will only execute if the Boolean expression after the *when* keyword evaluates to true. This is particularly useful for catching more than one exception type within a single catch block. The following code, for example, will only catch the exception if it matches either of the given types:

```
catch (Exception ex) when (ex is ArgumentOutOfRangeException ||
                           ex is ArgumentException)
```

Exception filters can contain any Boolean logical expression, with or without exception type matching. The following catch block will only execute if the exception type is ArgumentException and the *motorTemp* variable exceeds 102:

```
try
{
    VoltageCheck(501);
}
```

```
catch (Exception ex) when (ex is ArgumentOutOfRangeException && motorTemp > 102)
{
}
```

23.6 Using finally blocks

The purpose of the *finally* block is to specify code to be executed just before a *try-catch* statement finishes and is typically used to perform clean-up tasks, for example:

```
try
{
    VoltageCheck(501);
}
catch (Exception ex)
{
    Console.WriteLine(exception.Message);
}
finally
{
    Console.WriteLine("Resetting system.");
}
```

23.7 Using the try-finally Statement

From previous experience, we know that an unhandled exception will cause a running app to crash, but have yet to explain where exceptions can be caught and handled. The examples covered in this chapter so far have implied that exceptions must be handled at the point that they occur using a *try-catch* statement. In practice, however, this is not the case. Before exploring this topic in more detail it helps to view the execution path of a running app as a hierarchy of method calls, starting with the Main() method representing the top level.

Consider a scenario where the Main() method calls Method A which, in turn, calls methods B and C. Method C then calls Method D, and so on. This hierarchy of method calls is referred to as a *call tree* or *call hierarchy*. In diagram form, our theoretical call hierarchy might appear as shown in Figure 23-1 below:

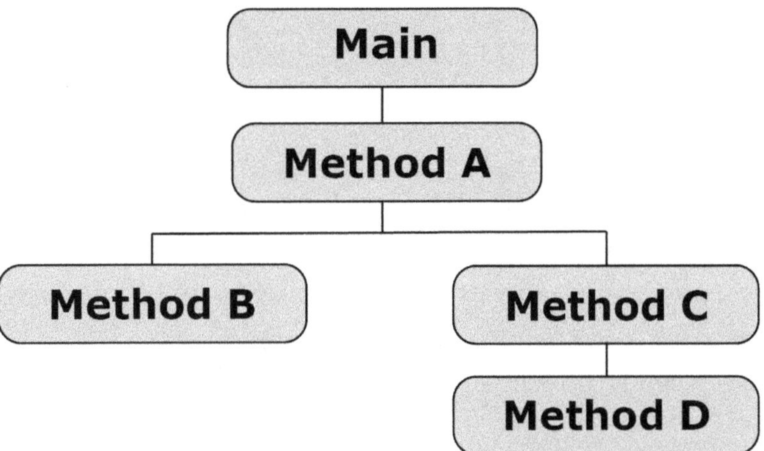

Figure 23-1

Suppose an exception is thrown in Method D. This exception will propagate up through the call hierarchy until the exception is handled. If the exception reaches the Main() method without being caught, the app will crash.

This means that even though the exception was thrown in Method D, we can handle it in any direct ancestor method up to and including Main() to prevent the app from crashing.

To experience this firsthand, add an interim method named StartMotor() between the Main() and VoltageCheck() methods and remove the *try-catch* statement:

```
namespace ExceptionDemo
{
    internal class Program
    {
        static void Main(string[] args)
        {
            StartMotor();
        }

        private static void StartMotor()
        {
            VoltageCheck(501);
            Console.WriteLine("Clean up after check.");
        }

        private static void VoltageCheck(int voltage)
        {
            if (voltage > 500)
            {
                throw new ArgumentOutOfRangeException(nameof(voltage),
                                    "Voltage exceeds safety parameters.");
            }
            else
            {
                Console.WriteLine("Safe Voltage");
            }
        }
    }
}
```

Since the exception is not caught in any of the three methods, the app will crash when it runs. We can, however, catch the error by adding a *try-catch* statement to VoltageCheck(), StartMotor() or Main(). For this example, use a *try-catch* statement to call StartMotor() from within the Main() method:

```
static void Main(string[] args)
{
    try
    {
        StartMotor();
    }
    catch (Exception ex) {
        Console.WriteLine(ex.Message);
```

```
    }
}
```

Rerun the app and confirm that the exception propagated up to the Main() method and was caught and handled:

```
Voltage exceeds safety parameters. (Parameter 'voltage')
```

Note that the above console output does not perform the cleanup operation after the voltage check. As currently implemented, StartMotor() will be unaware that the voltage check threw an exception and any code in StartMotor() after the VoltageCheck() will be skipped and control returned immediately to Main(). Suppose, however, that StartMotor needs to perform the cleanup after the voltage check, regardless of whether an exception was thrown. We can achieve this behavior using a *try-finally* statement:

```
private static void StartMotor()
{
    try
    {
        VoltageCheck(501);
    }
    finally
    {
        Console.WriteLine("Clean up whether or not voltage is safe.");
    }
}
```

Compile and run the app once more and verify that the cleanup occurs even when the exception is thrown:

```
Clean up whether or not voltage is safe.
Voltage exceeds safety parameters. (Parameter 'voltage')
```

23.8 Re-throwing exceptions

Sometimes an exception needs to be caught at multiple levels of the call hierarchy. This is achieved by *re-throwing* the exception after it has been caught so that it continues to pass upward in the hierarchy. Exceptions are re-thrown using the throw statement in the catch body as outlined below:

```
static void Main(string[] args)
{
    try
    {
        StartMotor();
    }
    catch (Exception ex) {
        Console.WriteLine("Caught in Main() " + ex.Message);
    }
}

private static void StartMotor()
{
    try
    {
        VoltageCheck(501);
    }
```

```
    catch (Exception ex)
    {
        Console.WriteLine("Caught in StartMotor " + ex.Message);
        throw;
    }
    finally
    {
        Console.WriteLine("Clean up whether or not voltage is safe.");
    }
}
```

Run the app and check the console to verify that the re-throw worked and that the exception was caught by both methods:

```
StartMotor(): Voltage exceeds safety parameters. (Parameter 'voltage')
Clean up whether or not voltage is safe.
Main(): Voltage exceeds safety parameters. (Parameter 'voltage')
```

23.9 Creating custom exception types

So far, this chapter has used built-in exception types to demonstrate how to throw and catch exceptions in C#. However, it will sometimes make more sense to create a custom exception type than using one of the predefined types. Custom types are derived from the Exception class and should include three constructors and parameters if required. The type name should also end in "Exception". The following code declares a custom exception type for high-voltage errors in our example app:

```
public class HighVoltageException : Exception
{
    public HighVoltageException()
    {
    }

    public HighVoltageException(string message)
        : base(message)
    {
    }

    public HighVoltageException(string message, Exception inner)
        : base(message, inner)
    {
    }
}
```

Once declared, the exception can be thrown as follows:

```
throw new HighVoltageException("Voltage exceeds safety parameters.");
```

The HighVoltageException type does not contain properties, so an instance can be created with only the message string:

```
throw new HighVoltageException("Voltage exceeds safety parameters.");
```

We can also extend the type declaration to include a property to record the voltage level when the exception occurred:

```
public class HighVoltageException : Exception
{
    public int Volts;

    public HighVoltageException()
    {
    }

    public HighVoltageException(string message)
        : base(message)
    {
    }

    public HighVoltageException(string message, Exception inner)
        : base(message, inner)
    {
    }

    public HighVoltageException(string message, int Volts)
        : base(message)
    {
        this.Volts = Volts;
    }
}
```

A HighVoltageException instance can now be created with a message string and the voltage value that triggered the exception:

```
private static void VoltageCheck(int voltage)
{
    if (voltage > 500)
    {
        throw new HighVoltageException("Voltage exceeds safety parameters.",
                                                                  voltage);
    }
    else
    {
        Console.WriteLine("Safe Voltage");
    }
}
```

Exception properties can be accessed from within catch blocks in the same way as the message property. In the following example, the Volts property is included in the notification text and used to make a decision based on the voltage level:

```
try
{
```

```
    StartMotor();
}
catch (HighVoltageException ex)
{
    Console.WriteLine(ex.Message);
    Console.Write("Current voltage: {ex.Volts}");

    if (ex.Volts < 510)
    {
        // Wait and retry
    }
    else
    {
        // Critical. Shutdown system
    }
}
```

23.10 Take the knowledge test

Click the link below or scan the QR code to test your knowledge and understanding of C# exception handling:

https://www.answertopia.com/hy8t

23.11 Summary

Exception handling in C# ensures that programs deal with errors effectively by allowing code to catch, handle, and respond to problems without crashing. Exceptions are "thrown" when a method encounters an error that prevents it from proceeding. Each exception has a specific type which provides information about the nature of the error. In addition to predefined exception types like ArgumentOutOfRangeException, custom exception types can be created when more specific error details are needed. Throwing an exception stops the normal flow of execution and transfers control to exception-handling code.

Exceptions are handled using *try-catch* blocks. The code that may throw an exception is placed inside the try block, while the catch block contains code to handle the exception if one is thrown. The catch block can access details about the exception, and in cases where multiple types of exceptions may occur, specific exception types can be handled separately using filtering. The *finally* block can also be used to execute code, such as cleaning up resources, whether or not an exception occurs.

Chapter 24

24. Asynchronous Programming in C#

Asynchronous programming allows software to execute multiple tasks simultaneously. This means tasks like downloading images or processing large amounts of data can be completed faster than if performed sequentially. Multi-tasking also provides a smoother user experience by allowing time-consuming operations to be performed in the background without impacting the app's responsiveness.

In this chapter, we will explore the asynchronous features of C# and explain how they can be used to incorporate multi-tasking support into your projects.

24.1 An overview of threads

Threads are a fundamental feature of modern CPUs and are essential for multitasking in operating systems. While CPUs can handle numerous threads, the actual number of threads that can run in parallel at a given time is limited by the number of CPU cores, typically ranging from 4 to 16 cores depending on the CPU model. When the number of threads exceeds the available CPU cores, the operating system uses thread scheduling to determine how these threads are shared among the available cores.

Threads are like small processes that run within a main process. They allow for the appearance of parallel execution within applications and managing them directly in code can be a complex and unpredictable process. The great thing about the asynchronous features of C#, however, is that they use threads behind the scenes, handling all the complexity for you.

24.2 The main thread

When an app is first started, the runtime system will typically create a single thread in which the app will run by default. Any code within an app that performs a time-consuming task using the main thread will cause the entire application to appear to lock up until the task is completed. This can be avoided by launching the tasks to be performed in separate threads, allowing the main thread to continue unhindered with other tasks.

24.3 Asynchronous programming in C#

Asynchronous support in C# is provided by the Task Asynchronous Programming model (TAP), which allows parallel execution to be performed safely and in a way that is logical and easy to both write and understand. In other words, asynchronous C# code is written sequentially from top to bottom in much the same way as synchronous, making it easy to understand the logic flow.

This chapter introduces C# asynchronous programming, providing in-depth coverage of key concepts and techniques for efficient parallel execution.

24.4 Creating the AsyncDemo project

Launch VS Code, open your "C# Essentials" workspace folder, and create a new .NET Console App project named AsyncDemo.

24.5 Synchronous code

Before exploring asynchronous programming, we will first look at an example of synchronous code execution. Begin by opening the *Program.cs* file and modifying it as follows:

```
namespace AsyncDemo
{
    internal class Program
    {
        static void Main(string[] args)
        {
        }

        private static string ProcessFile(string filename) {
            Console.WriteLine($"Start {filename} at {DateTime.Now}");
            Task.Delay(6000).Wait();
            return filename;
        }
    }
}
```

The ProcessFile() method outputs a starting timestamp before calling the Task.Delay() and Wait() methods to simulate a 6-second file processing task that blocks the current thread. After the delay, the method returns the name of the completed file.

Next, we want to call ProcessFile() multiple times from the Main() method. In doing so, we will also output start timestamps and use the C# Stopwatch diagnostic class to record the total execution time of the method calls:

```
using System.Diagnostics;

namespace AsyncDemo
{
    internal class Program
    {
        static void Main(string[] args)
        {
            Stopwatch stopwatch = Stopwatch.StartNew();

            Console.WriteLine("\n=== Before async task calls ===\n");

            string filename1 = ProcessFile("file1.txt");
            Console.WriteLine($"End   {filename1} at {DateTime.Now}\n");

            string filename2 = ProcessFile("file2.txt");
            Console.WriteLine($"End   {filename2} at {DateTime.Now}\n");

            string filename3 = ProcessFile("file3.txt");
            Console.WriteLine($"End   {filename3} at {DateTime.Now}\n");
```

```
            Console.WriteLine("=== After async tasks calls ===\n");

            stopwatch.Stop();
            TimeSpan timeSpan = stopwatch.Elapsed;
            Console.WriteLine($"Elapsed time: {timeSpan.Seconds} seconds");
        }
.
.
}
```

Run the app and check the console output resembles the following:

```
Start file1.txt at 9/24/2024 1:05:04 PM
End   file1.txt at 9/24/2024 1:05:10 PM

Start file2.txt at 9/24/2024 1:05:10 PM
End   file2.txt at 9/24/2024 1:05:16 PM

Start file3.txt at 9/24/2024 1:05:16 PM
End   file3.txt at 9/24/2024 1:05:22 PM

Elapsed time: 18 seconds
```

As we can see from the above output, the three calls to the ProcessFile() method were executed sequentially resulting in a combined processing time of 18 seconds. Converting ProcessFile() to an asynchronous method should reduce the total elapsed time from 18 to 6 seconds. Before we make this change, however, we first need to introduce the C# Task class.

24.6 Understanding the C# Task class

Asynchronous operations in C# are represented by Task objects. As we saw earlier, we can directly call static Task methods such as Delay(), for example:

```
Task.Delay(6000);
```

The above code will start an *asynchronous* 6-second delay. In other words, although the delay will be performed, it will occur in the background, and any subsequent code after the call will execute immediately. To make the execution block the current thread we called the Wait() method of the Task to prevent further execution until after the delay:

```
Task.Delay(6000).Wait();
```

As we will see in the remainder of this chapter, any asynchronous operation that we initiate will have a Task object associated with it that will allow us to manage the background execution.

24.7 Declaring asynchronous methods

Asynchronous execution can be applied to methods, lambdas, and anonymous functions and are declared using the *async* keyword and specifying a Task return type. C# naming convention also recommends, but does not require, that the method name ends in "Async". Given these requirements, we can modify our ProcessFile() method as follows:

```
private static async Task<string> ProcessFileAsync(string filename)
{
    Console.WriteLine($"Start {filename} at {DateTime.Now}");
```

```
    await Task.Delay(6000).Wait();
    return filename;
}
```

We have declared that the method is asynchronous and returns a Task object containing a string result parameter (in this case the file name).

Note that because we are now working within an async method, we have switched from calling the Wait() method of the Task object to using the await operator.

24.8 Introducing the await operator

The foundations of C# asynchronous execution are the Task class and the *await* operator. The await operator tells the system to suspend the execution of the calling method until a corresponding asynchronous operation completes and returns.

Using our AsyncDemo example, we know that the Main() method makes three consecutive calls to the file processing method and that each call has to wait until the previous one completes before it can execute. In addition to being an inefficient way to process multiple files, none of the code after the three calls can execute until the last one completes, essentially locking up the app. In all likelihood, there are other tasks the Main() method could be performing while waiting for the results to be returned from the ProcessFileAsync() method calls, such as processing other data, providing status updates to the user, and responding to user input.

Using Task objects and await, we can run three file processing operations in parallel and also allow other code in the Main() method to run while we wait for the results from the asynchronous calls.

As a first step, we will demonstrate why asynchronous execution requires both a Task object and the await operator. A point to note first, however, is that async methods can generally only be called from within the scope of other async methods (though, as we will see later in the chapter, the Task object can be used to provide a bridge between synchronous and asynchronous code). With this in mind, make the following changes to declare Main() as an asynchronous method:

```
static async Task Main(string[] args)
{
    Stopwatch stopwatch = Stopwatch.StartNew();
.
.
```

Next, modify the asynchronous calls to use the await operator as shown below:

```
static async Task Main(string[] args)
{
    Stopwatch stopwatch = Stopwatch.StartNew();

    Console.WriteLine("\n=== Before async task calls ===\n");

    string filename1 = await ProcessFileAsync("file1.txt");
    Console.WriteLine($"End   {filename1} at {DateTime.Now}\n");

    string filename2 = await ProcessFileAsync("file2.txt");
    Console.WriteLine($"End   {filename2} at {DateTime.Now}\n");

    string filename3 = await ProcessFileAsync("file3.txt");
```

```
    Console.WriteLine($"End   {filename3} at {DateTime.Now}");

    Console.WriteLine("\n=== After async tasks calls ===\n");

    stopwatch.Stop();
    TimeSpan timeSpan = stopwatch.Elapsed;
    Console.WriteLine($"Elapsed time: {timeSpan.Seconds} seconds\n");
}
```

Once the modifications are complete, run the app and check the console output, which resembles the following:

```
=== Before async task calls ===

Start file1.txt at 9/25/2024 9:53:46 AM
End   file1.txt at 9/25/2024 9:53:52 AM

Start file2.txt at 9/25/2024 9:53:52 AM
End   file2.txt at 9/25/2024 9:53:58 AM

Start file3.txt at 9/25/2024 9:53:58 AM
End   file3.txt at 9/25/2024 9:54:04 AM

=== After async tasks calls ===

Elapsed time: 18 seconds
```

Although we have made the file processing method asynchronous and used the await operator, the console output shows that the tasks are still being performed sequentially. By assigning the result from the await operation directly to the string variables we have committed ourselves to waiting until the result is returned, thereby forcing the code to execute synchronously.

To resolve this, we need to implement the following execution flow:

1. App launches.

2. Main() calls async methods.

3. Main() continues to execute while async tasks run in the background.

4. After completing other work, Main() suspends while awaiting results from async tasks.

5. Async tasks complete and return results.

6. Main() resumes execution.

The challenge is to obtain references to the async tasks that can be used later to await the results. We achieve this by storing the Task objects returned by the async methods and using them later in the code to await the results. To see this in action, make the following changes to the Main() method:

```
static async Task Main(string[] args)
{
    Stopwatch stopwatch = Stopwatch.StartNew();
```

```
    Console.WriteLine("\n=== Before async task calls ===\n");

    Task<string> task1 = ProcessFileAsync("file1.txt");
    Task<string> task2 = ProcessFileAsync("file2.txt");
    Task<string> task3 = ProcessFileAsync("file3.txt");

    Console.WriteLine("=== After async tasks calls ===\n");

    string filename1 = await task1;
    Console.WriteLine($"End   {filename1} at {DateTime.Now}");

    string filename2 = await task2;
    Console.WriteLine($"End   {filename2} at {DateTime.Now}");

    string filename3 = await task3;
    Console.WriteLine($"End   {filename3} at {DateTime.Now}\n");

    stopwatch.Stop();
    TimeSpan timeSpan = stopwatch.Elapsed;
    Console.WriteLine($"Elapsed time: {timeSpan.Seconds} seconds");
}
```

Rerun the app and check the console output:

```
=== Before async task calls ===

Start file1.txt at 9/25/2024 1:59:16 PM
Start file2.txt at 9/25/2024 1:59:16 PM
Start file3.txt at 9/25/2024 1:59:16 PM

=== After async tasks calls ===

End   file1.txt at 9/25/2024 1:59:22 PM
End   file2.txt at 9/25/2024 1:59:22 PM
End   file3.txt at 9/25/2024 1:59:22 PM

Elapsed time: 6 seconds
```

The first point to note from the above output is that the total execution time has dropped to 6 seconds from the previous 18 seconds because the three async tasks were executed concurrently. In addition, the "After async tasks calls" message appears before the async tasks have been completed, allowing Main() to perform other work before waiting for the task results.

As an alternative to waiting for each task to complete individually, we can pass them to the Task.WaitAll() method and obtain the return values via the Result property of the respective Task objects:

```
static async Task Main(string[] args)
{
.
```

```
.
    Console.WriteLine("\n=== After async tasks calls ===\n");

    Task.WaitAll(task1, task2, task3);

    Console.WriteLine($"End  {task1.Result} at {DateTime.Now}");
    Console.WriteLine($"End  {task2.Result} at {DateTime.Now}");
    Console.WriteLine($"End  {task3.Result} at {DateTime.Now}");
.
.
}
```

24.9 Asynchronous calls from synchronous functions

As previously mentioned, async methods are expected to be called from within an asynchronous context. It is, however, possible to start async tasks from within a synchronous context by calling the Task.Run() method. Suppose we have a synchronous method named *SyncMethod()* from which we need to call an async method and attempt to do so as follows:

```
private static void SyncMethod()
{
    await AsyncMethod();
}
```

The above code will result in the following error notification in the code editor:

```
The 'await' operator can only be used within an async method. Consider marking
this method with the 'async' modifier and changing its return type to 'Task'.
```

The only options we have are to make SyncMethod() an async method or start the task using the Task.Run() method. Assuming that declaring SyncMethod() as an async method is not a viable option, in this case, the code will need to be changed as follows:

```
private static void SyncMethod()
{
    Task.Run(async () => {
        await AsyncMethod();
    });
}
```

24.10 Canceling asynchronous tasks

Active asynchronous tasks can be canceled at any time using the CancellationTokenSource class. A CancellationTokenSource instance contains a unique CancellationToken object that is used to send cancellation requests to running tasks. To add cancellation support to the AsyncDemo project, begin with the following changes to the Main() method:

```
static async Task Main(string[] args)
{
    var tokenSource = new CancellationTokenSource();
    var cancellationToken = tokenSource.Token;
.
.
```

Now that we have a cancellation token, some changes need to be made to the ProcessFileAsync() method so that it can be passed to the Task that performs the 6-second delay:

```
private static async Task<string> ProcessFileAsync(string filename,
                                    CancellationToken cancellationToken)
{
    Console.WriteLine($"Start {filename} at {DateTime.Now}");
    await Task.Delay(6000, cancellationToken);

    return filename;
}
```

Before we can add code to send a cancellation request, some additional steps are required. As currently written, the app will crash when the task is canceled with console output that will read in part:

```
Unhandled exception. System.AggregateException: One or more errors occurred. (A
task was canceled.)
 ---> System.Threading.Tasks.TaskCanceledException: A task was canceled.
   at System.Threading.Tasks.Task.GetExceptions(Boolean
includeTaskCanceledExceptions)
```

The problem here is that when a task is canceled it triggers an exception which, if not handled correctly by the app, will result in a crash. The solution to this is to configure the token to throw an OperationCanceledException error when the task is canceled, and then use a *try-catch* statement to gracefully handle the exception:

```
private static async Task<string> ProcessFileAsync(string filename,
CancellationToken cancellationToken)
{

    Console.WriteLine($"Start {filename} at {DateTime.Now}");

    try
    {
        cancellationToken.ThrowIfCancellationRequested();
        await Task.Delay(6000, cancellationToken);
    }
    catch (OperationCanceledException)
    {
        Console.WriteLine($"{filename} processing cancelled");
    }

    return filename;
}
```

In the above example, we just output a message indicating the task has been canceled, but in a real-world app, this is where steps can be taken to clean up, such as removing temporary files or closing network connections.

The final step is to provide a way for the user to cancel the async tasks. We do this by calling the Cancel() method of the CancellationTokenSource object:

```
tokenSource.Cancel();
```

To demonstrate canceling the file processing tasks, we will add code after the tasks have been launched to cancel the tasks when a key is pressed as follows:

```
static async Task Main(string[] args)
{
    var tokenSource = new CancellationTokenSource();
    var cancellationToken = tokenSource.Token;
.
.
    Console.WriteLine("\n=== After async tasks calls ===\n");

    Console.Write("Press any key to cancel");
    Console.ReadKey();
    tokenSource.Cancel();

    Task.WaitAll(task1, task2, task3);
.
.
```

Rerun the app, click in the console window, and tap any key within 6 seconds to cancel the tasks. The console output should indicate that the cancellation exception was handled cleanly and that the tasks were canceled before completing their work:

```
=== Before async task calls ===

Start file1.txt at 9/26/2024 2:15:04 PM
Start file2.txt at 9/26/2024 2:15:04 PM
Start file3.txt at 9/26/2024 2:15:04 PM

=== After async tasks calls ===

Press any key to cancel
file3.txt processing canceled
file2.txt processing canceled
file1.txt processing canceled
End   file1.txt at 9/26/2024 2:15:06 PM
End   file2.txt at 9/26/2024 2:15:06 PM
End   file3.txt at 9/26/2024 2:15:06 PM
Elapsed time: 1 seconds
```

24.11 Take the knowledge test

Click the link below or scan the QR code to test your knowledge and understanding of C# asynchronous programming:

https://www.answertopia.com/akfm

24.12 Summary

Asynchronous programming in C# uses the Task class and await operator to run tasks in parallel, improving performance and responsiveness. The await operator suspends execution until a task is completed, allowing other code to run concurrently. By converting synchronous methods to asynchronous ones, multiple tasks can be executed simultaneously, reducing overall execution time.

To achieve concurrent execution, store Task objects returned by async methods and await their results later. Cancellation of asynchronous tasks can be implemented using the Cancel() method of the CancellationTokenSource object. When canceling tasks, appropriate steps should be taken to handle exceptions to prevent the app from crashing.

Chapter 25

25. Creating 2D, 3D, and Jagged Arrays in C#

Arrays are certainly not unique to C#. In fact, just about every other programming and scripting language preceding the introduction of C# provided support for arrays. An array allows a collection of values of the same type to be stored and accessed via a single variable. Each item is accessed in the array variable through the use of an array index.

C# arrays, while useful, have some limitations. Perhaps the most significant limitation is the fact that once an array has been created, it cannot be made larger or smaller to accommodate more or fewer values. More dynamic and flexible collection storage capabilities will be covered starting with the chapter titled *"C# List Collections"*.

25.1 Creating arrays in C#

A C# array may be created in several different ways. One way is to declare an array without initializing it with any values. The syntax for this is as follows:

```
type[] arrayname;
```

In the above example, type represents the type of data to be stored in the array (for example, string, int, decimal etc). The square brackets ([]) indicate that this is the declaration for an array, and *arrayname* is the name by which the array is to be referred.

For example, we can declare an array of strings called *myColors* as follows:

```
string[] myColors;
```

In this example, we have declared the array but not assigned any values to it. To assign values after an array has been declared, use the following syntax:

```
string[] myColors;
myColors = ["red", "green", "yellow", "orange", "blue"];
```

An array may also be initialized in the declaration line simply by placing the comma-separated list of values after the declaration:

```
string[] myColors = ["red", "green", "yellow", "orange", "blue"];
```

Another option is to declare the size of the array when it is created. For example, to declare an array of size 5, place the size value within the square brackets of the *new* statement:

```
string[] myColors = new string[5];
```

This will reserve the space required for the full array without actually placing any values into the array. The array elements may be initialized at creation as follows (note that the number of elements must match the size specified):

```
string[] myColors = new string[5] { "red", "green", "yellow", "orange", "blue" };
```

25.2 Declaring multidimensional arrays

Multidimensional arrays are declared by placing commas within the square brackets. For example, to declare a two-dimensional array:

Creating 2D, 3D, and Jagged Arrays in C#

```
char[,] my2Darray;
```

The single comma (,) in the above syntax indicates to C# that this is to a two-dimensional array. A two-dimensional array is initialized as follows:

```
char[,] my2Darray =
{
    {'a', 'b', 'c'},
    {'c', 'd', 'e'},
    {'c', 'd', 'e'}
};
```

This creates a multidimensional array containing three rows and three columns.

When the array was declared above, the task of inferring the array dimensions was left to the C# compiler. These dimensions may also be specified when the array is declared using the *new* statement, for example:

```
char[,] my2Darray = new char[3,3]
{
    {'a', 'b', 'c'},
    {'c', 'd', 'e'},
    {'c', 'd', 'e'}
};
```

The following, on the other hand, declares a three-dimensional array:

```
int[,,] my3Darray;
```

The following code will initialize the three-dimensional array:

```
char[,,] my3Darray =
{
    {
        { 'a', 'b', 'c' },
        { 'c', 'd', 'e' }
    },
    {
        { 'f', 'g', 'h' },
        { 'i', 'j', 'k' }
    }
};
```

A three-dimensional array is essentially an array where each element is a two-dimensional array. In the above declaration, the array consists of two arrays, each of which contains a two-dimensional array, each containing three elements. This translates to an array with three dimensions of 2, 2, and 3.

It is also possible to specify the dimensions when the array is declared as follows:

```
char[,,] my3Darray2 = new char[2,2,3]
{
    {
        { 'a', 'b', 'c' },
        { 'c', 'd', 'e' }
    },
```

```
    {
        { 'f', 'g', 'h' },
        { 'i', 'j', 'k' }
    }
};
```

25.3 Declaring jagged arrays

A jagged array is an array where each element is itself an array. The term jagged is used in this context because the array elements can be of different lengths. A jagged array can be thought of as a 2D array where each array can have a different number of elements.

The following is an example of a declaration for a jagged array designed to hold two-dimensional arrays of variable sizes:

```
char[][] myJaggedArray;
```

The following code declares and initializes the same jagged array:

```
char[][] myJaggedArray =
[
    ['a', 'b', 'c', 'd', 'e'],
    ['f', 'g', 'h', 'i'],
    ['j', 'j'],
    ['k', 'l', 'm', 'n', 'o', 'p', 'q', 'r']
];
```

25.4 Take the knowledge test

Click the link below or scan the QR code to test your knowledge and understanding of C# arrays:

https://www.answertopia.com/e6ca

25.5 Summary

C# arrays allow collections of values of the same type, with each item accessed through an index. Multidimensional arrays are declared with commas within square brackets, while jagged arrays are arrays of arrays with varying lengths.

Chapter 26

26. Accessing and Sorting C# Array Elements

The previous chapter explained how to create 2-dimensional, 3-dimensional, and jagged arrays in C#. In this chapter, we will explore how to access, remove, and sort the elements of an array.

26.1 Creating the ArrayDemo Project

Launch VS Code, open your "C# Essentials" workspace folder and create a new .NET Console App project named ArrayDemo.

Once you have created the project, open the *Program.cs* file and use it to try out the examples in the rest of this chapter.

26.2 Getting the number of dimensions of an array

The number of dimensions of an array can be obtained via the Rank property of the array. For example:

```
char[,] my2Darray = new char[3,3]
{
   {'a', 'b', 'c'},
   {'c', 'd', 'e'},
   {'c', 'd', 'e'}
};

char[,,] my3Darray = new char[2,2,3]
{
   {
       { 'a', 'b', 'c' },
       { 'c', 'd', 'e' }
   },
   {
       { 'f', 'g', 'h' },
       { 'i', 'j', 'k' }
   }
};

Console.WriteLine($"Dimensions in my2Darray = {my2Darray.Rank}");
Console.WriteLine($"Dimensions in my3Darray = {my3Darray.Rank}");
```

Output:

```
Dimensions in my2Darray = 2
Dimensions in my3Darray = 3
```

26.3 Accessing array elements

Once values have been stored in an array, it is highly likely that these values will need to be accessed at some later point in the C# code. This is achieved using the array accessor notation combined with the index into the array of the desired value. The array accessor is simply the array name followed by square brackets ([]). Within the square brackets is placed a number representing the index into the array of the desired value (keeping in mind that the first array element in C# is index 0). For example, to access the second element of our myColors array, the following notation would be used:

```
string[] myColors = {"red", "green", "yellow", "orange", "blue"};

Console.WriteLine($"Element at index 1 = {myColors[1]}");
```

When executed, the above code will output the word "green" since this is the string contained at index position 1 in the array.

Similarly, the value at a particular index position in an array may be changed using the accessor notation combined with the assignment operator (=). For example, to change the value of the first item in the array:

```
string[] myColors = ["red", "green", "yellow", "orange", "blue"];

myColors[0] = "violet";
Console.WriteLine($"Element at index 0 = {myColors[0]}");
```

Values in a multidimensional array may be accessed by specifying the index values for each dimension separated by commas. For example, to access the first element of the first array of our my2Darray the following accessor would be used (keeping in mind that arrays start at index position 0):

```
char element = my2Darray[0,0];
```

The following code demonstrates accessing a variety of elements, both in 2D and 3D arrays:

```
char[,] my2Darray = new char[3,3]
{
   {'a', 'b', 'c'},
   {'d', 'e', 'f'},
   {'g', 'h', 'i'}
};

char[,,] my3Darray =
{
   {
       { 'a', 'b', 'c' },
       { 'd', 'e', 'f' }
   },
   {
       { 'g', 'h', 'i' },
       { 'j', 'k', 'l' }
   }
};

// Output first element of first array in my2Darray
```

```
Console.WriteLine($"{my2Darray[0,0]}");

// Output last element of last array in my2Darray
Console.WriteLine($"{my2Darray[2,2]}");

// Output 2nd element of 2nd array in 1st 2D array of my3Darray
Console.WriteLine($"{my3Darray[0,1,1]}");

// Output 3rd element of 2nd array in 2nd 2D array of my3Darray
Console.WriteLine($"{my3Darray[1,1,2]}");
```

Output:

```
a
i
e
l
```

26.4 Array iteration

The easiest way to iterate through the items in an array is to make use of the *foreach* looping syntax. The following code, for example, iterates through all of the items in an array and outputs each item to the console panel:

```
string[] myColors = ["red", "green", "yellow", "orange", "blue"];

foreach (string color in myColors)
{
    Console.Write("{0} ", color);
}
```

Output:

```
red green yellow orange blue
```

You can also use the *foreach* statement to iterate through multidimensional arrays. In the following example, we use *foreach* to iterate through all the elements of a three-dimensional array:

```
char[,,] my3Darray =
{
   {
       { 'a', 'b', 'c' },
       { 'c', 'd', 'e' }
   },
   {
       { 'f', 'g', 'h' },
       { 'i', 'j', 'k' }
   }
};

foreach (char letter in my3Darray)
{
    Console.Write("{0} ", letter);
```

```
}
```

Output:

```
a b c c d e f g h i j k
```

26.5 Working with ranges

The C# range (..) and index from end (^) operators are particularly useful for accessing subsets of array elements. Ranges are constructed using the following syntax where x and y represent the beginning and end range values, respectively:

```
x..y
```

When working with ranges, it is important to remember that range syntax x..y encompasses all the numbers from x up to, but not including, y. The range operator 5…8, therefore, specifies the positions 5, 6, and 7.

In the absence of start or end positions, the range will include all possible values starting at 0 until the end of the array is reached:

```
..
```

One-sided range operators specify a range that can extend as far as possible in a specified range direction until the natural beginning or end of the range is reached (or until some other condition is met). A one-sided range is declared by omitting the number from one side of the range declaration, for example:

```
x...
```

or

```
...y
```

A range to specify two elements in an array starting with position 2 through to the last element could be declared as follows:

```
2...
```

Similarly, to specify a range that begins with the first element and ends with the element at position 5, the range would be specified as follows:

```
...6
```

The following example extracts items 4 through 6 and assigns them to a new array named words:

```
string[] sentence = ["The", "best", "way", "to", "predict", "the", "future",
"is", "to", "invent", "it"];
string[] words = sentence[4..7];
```

Similarly, we can use the following range syntax to extract words starting at element 0 and ending at element 4:

```
string[] words = sentence[..5];
```

We can also combine the index operator with the range operator to perform operations similar to the following which extracts elements starting at position 1 up until the second from last element of the array:

```
string[] words = sentence[1..^2];
```

Try the following code to see the above examples in action:

```
string[] sentence = ["The", "best", "way", "to", "predict", "the", "future",
"is", "to", "invent", "it"];

string[] subset1 = sentence[^7..^4];
string[] subset2 = sentence[..^2];
```

```
string[] subset3 = sentence[3..^3];

foreach (string word in subset1)
{
    Console.Write("{0} ", word);
}

Console.WriteLine("\n");

foreach (string word in subset2)
{
    Console.Write("{0} ", word);
}

Console.WriteLine("\n");

foreach (string word in subset3)
{
    Console.Write("{0} ", word);
}

Console.WriteLine("\n");
```

When the above code runs, it will generate the following output:

```
predict the future
The best way to predict the future is to
to predict the future is
```

26.6 C# index from end operator

The C# index from end (^) operator allows you to specify the end of a range based on the number of positions from the end of the array.

The index ^1, for example, represents the last item in the array, ^2 the second from last item in the array, and so on. Index ^0 is already set to the total number of items in the array:

```
string[] myArray = {
    "item 1",   // <-- ^7 - 7th from last
    "item 2",   // <-- ^6
    "item 3",   // <-- ^5
    "item 4",   // <-- ^4
    "item 5",   // <-- ^3
    "item 6",   // <-- ^2
    "item 7"    // <-- ^1 - Last item
                // ^0 = array length
};
```

The following code demonstrates the use of the index operator when working with ranges and arrays:

```
string[] sentence = {"The", "best", "way", "to", "predict", "the", "future",
```

```
"is", "to", "invent", "it"};

string[] subset1 = sentence[^7..^4];
string[] subset2 = sentence[..^2];
string[] subset3 = sentence[3..^3];

foreach (string word in subset1)
{
    Console.Write("{0} ", word);
}

Console.WriteLine("\n");

foreach (string word in subset2)
{
    Console.Write("{0} ", word);
}

Console.WriteLine("\n");

foreach (string word in subset3)
{
    Console.Write("{0} ", word);
}
```

Output:

```
predict the future
The best way to predict the future is to
to predict the future is
```

26.7 Sorting C# arrays

The C# array is part of the Array package, which also includes some useful methods for sorting and re-ordering arrays.

If you need to sort an array, pass it as an argument to the Array.Sort() method as follows:

```
string[] myColors = [ "red", "green", "yellow", "orange", "blue" ];

Console.WriteLine("Before Sort");

foreach (string color in myColors)
{
    Console.Write("{0} ", color);
}

Array.Sort(myColors);

Console.WriteLine("\n\nAfter Sort");
```

```
foreach (string color in myColors)
{
    Console.Write("{0} ", color);
}
```

Output:

```
Before Sort
red green yellow orange blue

After Sort
blue green orange red yellow
```

You can also reverse the order of the elements in an array using the Array.Reverse() method:

```
string[] myColors = ["red", "green", "yellow", "orange", "blue"];

Array.Reverse(myColors);

foreach (string color in myColors)
{
    Console.Write("{0} ", color);
}
```

Output:

```
blue orange yellow green red
```

26.8 Clearing C# arrays

The values in an array may be cleared using the Array.Clear() method. This method clears each item in an array to the default value for the type (false for Boolean values, 0 for numeric items, and null for strings). The syntax for clearing array elements is as follows:

```
Array.Clear(<array>, <start index>, <count>);
```

In the above syntax, <array> is the array to be cleared, <start index> is the position within the array at which clearing is to begin, and <count> is the number of elements to be cleared.

The following example clears three elements starting at item 1:

```
string[] myColors = ["red", "green", "yellow", "orange", "blue"];

Array.Clear(myColors, 1, 3);

foreach (string color in myColors)
{
    Console.Write("{0} ", color);
}
```

When the above code runs, only the blue and red elements will remain in the array.

26.9 Take the knowledge test

Click the link below or scan the QR code to test your knowledge and understanding of C# array management:

https://www.answertopia.com/ty5r

26.10 Summary

This chapter explored accessing, removing, and sorting elements in C# arrays. It demonstrated how to use the Rank property to determine the number of dimensions, the array accessor notation to access elements, and the *foreach* loop to iterate through arrays. Additionally, it covers using ranges and the index from end operator to extract subsets of elements, and the Array.Sort(), Array.Reverse(), and Array.Clear() methods to sort, reverse, and clear arrays, respectively.

Chapter 27

27. C# List Collections

In the previous chapters, we looked at C# Arrays. While useful for many tasks, arrays are starting to show their age in terms of functionality and flexibility. The C# Collection Classes provide more advanced mechanisms for gathering groups of objects.

27.1 Creating the CollectionDemo Project

Launch VS Code, open your "C# Essentials" workspace folder and create a new .NET Console App project named CollectionDemo.

Once you have created the project, open the *Program.cs* file and use it to try out the examples in the rest of this chapter.

27.2 Introducing the C# Collection Classes

The C# Collection classes are designed specifically for grouping objects and performing tasks on them. Several collection classes are available with C#, and we will look at some key classes in the next few chapters.

27.3 Creating C# list collections with List<T>

The List<T> class has properties very similar to C# arrays. One key advantage of this class over arrays is that it can grow and shrink as the number of stored objects changes.

The syntax for creating a List<T> collection is as follows where type is replaced by the data type to be stored in the list:

```
List<type> name = new List<type>();
```

Alternatively, the above syntax may be simplified as follows:

```
List<type> name = [];
```

With the above syntax in mind, we could create an empty List<T> object named *colorList* configured to store string values using either of the following statements:

```
List<string> colorList = new List<string>();
List<string> colorList = [];
```

27.4 Adding items to lists

Once you have created a List object instance, there are several methods you can call to perform tasks on the list. One such method is the Add() method which, as the name suggests, is used to add items to the list object:

```
List<string> colorList = [];
colorList.Add ("Red");
colorList.Add ("Green");
colorList.Add ("Yellow");
colorList.Add ("Purple");
colorList.Add ("Orange");
```

The Add() method appends the new item to the end of the list. To insert new items at a specific index location, you will need to use the Insert() method covered later in the chapter.

27.5 Initializing a list with multiple values

In the above example, we created an empty list and then added items one by one using the Add() method. However, if you need to initialize a list with a large number of values, you may find it more efficient to use a collection initializer, the syntax for which is as follows:

```
List<type> <list-name> = [ <item1>, <item2>, <item3>, ... ]
```

Using this syntax, we can modify our initialization example as follows:

```
List<string> colorList = ["Red", "Green", "Yellow", "Purple", "Orange"];
```

27.6 Accessing list items

Individual items in a list may be accessed using the item's index value (keeping in mind that the first item is index 0, the second index 1, and so on). The index value is placed in square brackets after the list name. For example, to access the second item in the *colorList* object:

```
List<string> colorList = ["Red", "Green", "Yellow", "Purple", "Orange"];

Console.WriteLine(colorList[1]);
```

Output:

```
Green
```

A list item value can similarly be changed using the index combined with the assignment (=) operator. For example, to change the Yellow color to Indigo, the code would read as follows:

```
List<string> colorList = ["Red", "Green", "Yellow", "Purple", "Orange"];

Console.WriteLine($"Color before = {colorList[2]}");
colorList[2] = "Indigo";
Console.WriteLine($"Color after = {colorList[2]}");
```

Output:

```
Color before = Yellow
Color after = Indigo
```

As with arrays, you can also construct a *foreach* loop to list all of the items in a list. For example:

```
List<string> colorList = ["Red", "Green", "Yellow", "Purple", "Orange"];

foreach (string color in colorList)
{
    Console.Write($"{color} ");
}
```

Output:

```
Red Green Yellow Purple Orange
```

27.7 Removing items from lists

Items may be removed from a list using the Remove() method. This method takes the value of the item to be removed as an argument. For example, to remove the "Orange" string from the *colorList* object, we could write the following code:

```
List<string> colorList = ["Red", "Green", "Yellow", "Purple", "Orange"];
```

```
colorList.Remove("Orange");

foreach (string color in colorList)
{
    Console.Write($"{color} ");
}
```

Output:

```
Green Yellow Purple Orange
```

Note that C# lists can store duplicate entries. In the case of duplicated items, the Remove() method will only remove the first matching instance.

27.8 Inserting items into a list

Previously we used the Add() method to add items to a list. The Add() method, however, only adds items to the end of a list. Sometimes it is necessary to insert a new item at a specific location in a list. The Insert() method is provided for this particular purpose.

Insert() takes two arguments, an integer indicating the index location of the insertion and the item to be inserted at that location. For example, to insert an item at location 2 in our example list:

```
List<string> colorList = ["Red", "Green", "Yellow", "Purple", "Orange"];
colorList.Insert(2, "White");

foreach (string color in colorList)
{
    Console.Write($"{color} ");
}
```

Output:

```
Red Green White Yellow Purple Orange
```

27.9 Sorting lists in C#

There is no way to tell C# to automatically sort a list as items are added. The items in a list can be sorted into order by calling the Sort() method:

```
List<string> colorList = ["Red", "Green", "Yellow", "Purple", "Orange"];

colorList.Sort();

foreach (string color in colorList)
{
    Console.Write($"{color} ");
}
```

Output:

```
Green Orange Purple Red Yellow
```

The above example uses the C# default comparison delegate to organize the new list order. Although beyond the scope of this book, it is worth knowing that for more advanced requirements, you can create your own comparison delegate.

27.10 Finding items in a C# list

Several methods are provided with the List class for finding items. The most basic method is the Contains() method which, when called on a list object, returns true if the specified item is located in the list, or false if it is not.

The IndexOf() method returns the index value of a matching item in a list. For example, the following code sample will output a true result indicating the presence of "Red" and the value 2, which is the index position of the "Yellow" string:

```
List<string> colorList = ["Red", "Green", "Yellow", "Purple", "Orange"];

Console.WriteLine(colorList.Contains("Red"));
Console.WriteLine(colorList.IndexOf("Yellow"));
```

Output:

```
True
2
```

If the item is not found in the list, a value of -1 is returned by the IndexOf() method.

The LastIndexOf() method returns the index value of the last item in the list to match the specified item. This is particularly useful when a list contains duplicate items:

```
List<string> colorList = ["Red", "Green", "Yellow", "Purple", "Red"];

Console.WriteLine(colorList.LastIndexOf("Red"));
```

Output:

```
4
```

27.11 Obtaining information about a list

Two properties of the List<T> class are helpful in obtaining information about a list object. For example, the Capacity property can identify how many items a collection can store without resizing.

The Count property, however, identifies how many items are currently stored in the list. In general, the Capacity value will match or exceed the current Count:

```
List<string> colorList = ["Red", "Green", "Yellow", "Purple", "Orange"];

Console.WriteLine($"Count = {colorList.Count}");
Console.WriteLine($"Capacity = {colorList.Capacity}");
```

Output:

```
Count = 5
Capacity = 5
```

In instances where a gap exists between Count and Capacity you can remove excess capacity with a call the TrimExcess() method:

```
colorList.TrimExcess();
```

27.12 Clearing C# lists

You can remove all of the items in a list by making a call to the Clear() method.

The Clear() method removes the items from the list and sets the Count property to zero. The Capacity property, however, remains unchanged after the list has been cleared. To remove the capacity of a list, follow the Clear() method call with a call to TrimExcess():

```
List<string> colorList = ["Red", "Green", "Yellow", "Purple", "Orange"];

Console.WriteLine($"Count = {colorList.Count}");
Console.WriteLine($"Capacity = {colorList.Capacity}");

colorList.Clear();

Console.WriteLine($"Count = {colorList.Count}");
Console.WriteLine($"Capacity = {colorList.Capacity}");

colorList.TrimExcess();

Console.WriteLine($"Count = {colorList.Count}");
Console.WriteLine($"Capacity = {colorList.Capacity}");
```

Output:

```
Count = 5
Capacity = 5
Count = 0
Capacity = 5
Count = 0
Capacity = 0
```

27.13 Take the knowledge test

Click the link below or scan the QR code to test your knowledge and understanding of C# List collections:

https://www.answertopia.com/tccy

27.14 Summary

C# Collection Classes provide advanced mechanisms for grouping objects, with List<T> being a key class that allows for dynamic resizing. Lists can be created, modified, and queried using methods like Add(), Remove(), Contains(), and IndexOf(). Additionally, lists can be sorted, cleared, and their properties like Count and Capacity can be accessed to obtain information about the list content.

Chapter 28

28. C# Dictionary Collections

C# dictionaries allow data to be stored and managed as key-value pairs. Dictionaries fulfill a similar purpose to arrays and lists, except each item stored in the dictionary has associated with it a unique key (to be precise, the key is unique to the particular dictionary object) which can be used to reference and access the corresponding value.

28.1 Creating the DictionaryDemo Project

Launch VS Code, open your "C# Essentials" workspace folder and create a new .NET Console App project named DictionaryDemo.

Once you have created the project, open the *Program.cs* file and use it to try out the examples in the rest of this chapter.

28.2 Dictionary initialization

A dictionary is a data type explicitly designed to hold multiple values in a single unordered collection. Each item in a dictionary consists of a key and an associated value.

An empty dictionary may be created using the following syntax:

```
Dictionary<key-type, value-type> name =
    new Dictionary<key-type, value-type>();
```

The following code, for example, creates an empty dictionary using an int for the key and a string for the values:

```
Dictionary<int, string> movies =
    new Dictionary<int, string>();
```

Alternatively, you can use implicit typing using the var keyword:

```
var movies = new Dictionary<int, string>();
```

A new dictionary may be initialized with a collection of values using a collection initializer with the following syntax (note that we are once again using implicit typing):

```
var name = new Dictionary<key-type, value-type>()
{
    { key1, value1 },
    { key2, value2 },
    { key3, value3 },
.
.
};
```

The following code creates a new dictionary initialized with four key-value pairs in the form of strings acting as keys for corresponding movie titles:

```
var movies = new Dictionary<string, string>()
{
    { "DRA-1212", "The Godfather" },
```

```
    { "WAR-4433", "Apocalypse Now" },
    { "COM-5465", "The Terminal" },
    { "CLA-1659", "Casablanca" }
};
```

In the above instance, the C# compiler will use implicit typing to decide that both the key and value elements of the dictionary are of string and prevent values or keys of other types from being inserted into the dictionary.

28.3 Dictionary item count

A count of the items in a dictionary can be obtained by accessing the dictionary's Count property:

```
var movies = new Dictionary<string, string>()
    {
        { "DRA-1212", "The Godfather" },
        { "WAR-4433", "Apocalypse Now" },
        { "COM-5465", "The Terminal" },
        { "CLA-1659", "Casablanca" }
    };

Console.WriteLine($"Count = {movies.Count}");
```

Output:

```
Count = 4
```

28.4 Dictionary iteration

As with arrays and lists, you can iterate through all entries in a dictionary using *foreach* looping syntax. The following code, for example, iterates through all of the entries in the movies dictionary, outputting both the key and value for each entry:

```
var movies = new Dictionary<string, string>()
{
    { "DRA-1212", "The Godfather" },
    { "WAR-4433", "Apocalypse Now" },
    { "COM-5465", "The Terminal" },
    { "CLA-1659", "Casablanca" }
};

foreach (var movie in movies) {

    var key = movie.Key;
    var value = movie.Value;

    Console.WriteLine($"{key} - {value}");
}
```

Output:

```
DRA-1212 - The Godfather
WAR-4433 - Apocalypse Now
COM-5465 - The Terminal
```

```
CLA-1659 - Casablanca
```

As we can see in the above code, each entry within a dictionary has Key and Value properties. In this case, we have used these properties to extract each dictionary entry's key and movie title.

28.5 Adding and removing dictionary entries

New entries can be added to an existing dictionary by making a call to the Add() method of the instance, passing through the key/value pair:

```
var movies = new Dictionary<string, string>()
{
    { "DRA-1212", "The Godfather" },
    { "WAR-4433", "Apocalypse Now" },
    { "COM-5465", "The Terminal" },
    { "CLA-1659", "Casablanca" }
};

movies.Add("SCI-2323", "Prometheus");

Console.WriteLine(movies["SCI-2323"]);
```

Output:

```
Prometheus
```

You can remove an entry from a dictionary by calling the Remove() method, referencing the key matching the entry to be removed:

```
var movies = new Dictionary<string, string>()
{
    { "DRA-1212", "The Godfather" },
    { "WAR-4433", "Apocalypse Now" },
    { "COM-5465", "The Terminal" },
    { "CLA-1659", "Casablanca" }
};

movies.Remove("WAR-4433");

foreach (var movie in movies) {

    var key = movie.Key;
    var value = movie.Value;

    Console.WriteLine($"{key} - {value}");
}
```

Output:

```
DRA-1212 - The Godfather
COM-5465 - The Terminal
CLA-1659 - Casablanca
```

28.6 Accessing and updating dictionary items

A specific value may be accessed or modified using key subscript syntax to reference the corresponding value. The following code references a key known to be in the movies dictionary and outputs the associated value (in this case, the movie entitled "The Terminal"):

```
var movies = new Dictionary<string, string>()
{
    { "DRA-1212", "The Godfather" },
    { "WAR-4433", "Apocalypse Now" },
    { "COM-5465", "The Terminal" },
    { "CLA-1659", "Casablanca" }
};

Console.WriteLine(movies["COM-5465"]);
```

Output:

```
The Terminal
```

Indexing by key may also be used when updating the value associated with a specified key, for example, to change the title of the same movie from "The Terminal" to "Caddyshack"):

```
var movies = new Dictionary<string, string>()
{
    { "DRA-1212", "The Godfather" },
    { "WAR-4433", "Apocalypse Now" },
    { "COM-5465", "The Terminal" },
    { "CLA-1659", "Casablanca" }
};

movies["COM-5465"] = "Caddyshack";

Console.WriteLine(movies["COM-5465"]);
```

Output:

```
Caddyshack
```

28.7 Checking if a key or value exists

A dictionary can be searched to find out if it contains a particular key by calling the ContainsKey() method. Before adding new entries to a dictionary, you may want to call this method to ensure the key has not already been used to avoid a runtime exception error.

You can also check whether a specific value exists in a dictionary with a call to the ContainsValue() method. The following example demonstrates both of these methods in action:

```
var movies = new Dictionary<string, string>()
{
    { "DRA-1212", "The Godfather" },
    { "WAR-4433", "Apocalypse Now" },
    { "COM-5465", "The Terminal" },
    { "CLA-1659", "Casablanca" }
```

```
};

if (movies.ContainsKey("CLA-1659")) {
    Console.WriteLine("Key exists in dictionary");
}

if (movies.ContainsValue("The Godfather")) {
    Console.WriteLine("Title exists in dictionary");
}
```

Output:

```
Key exists in dictionary
Title exists in dictionary
```

28.8 Take the knowledge test

Click the link below or scan the QR code to test your knowledge and understanding of C# dictionary collections:

https://www.answertopia.com/mdz6

28.9 Summary

C# dictionaries store key-value pairs, allowing efficient data management. They can be initialized with collections or created empty. Dictionaries support iteration, adding/removing entries, and accessing/updating values using keys.

Chapter 29

29. C# File and Directory Handling

In this chapter, we explore how to work with files and directories in C#, covering classes and methods available in the System.IO namespace. In particular, we will use Directory, File, FileInfo, and Stream classes to handle files and work with filesystem directories. After completing this chapter, you'll be able to check if files exist, and create, read from, and write to text and binary files.

29.1 Introducing the System.IO classes

When we work with files and directories in C#, we do so using a set of classes provided by the System.IO namespace. The key classes, and the ones we will be using in this chapter, are as follows:

- **Path** - Provides a set of methods for managing file path strings, including constructing new paths and obtaining information about existing paths.
- **Directory** - Provides a set of static methods for creating, deleting, moving, and navigating filesystem directory structures.
- **DirectoryInfo** - Provides a set of features similar to the Directory class but in the form of non-static methods. This involves creating a DirectoryInfo instance initialized with the directory path and then calling methods on that object.
- **File** - Includes a set of static methods for working with files, including methods to create, copy, delete, and open files. The File static methods are passed paths to the files on which the corresponding action is to be performed.
- **FileInfo** - Provides features similar to the File class but in the form of non-static methods. This involves creating a FileInfo instance initialized with the file path and then calling methods on that object to perform operations such as opening, deleting, reading, and writing.
- **StreamReader / StreamWriter** - The StreamReader and StreamWriter classes provide a more flexible alternative to the File and FileInfo classes for reading from and writing to files. These classes are intended for use when working with text-based files.
- **BinaryReader / BinaryWriter** - These classes perform the same function as StreamReader and StreamWriter classes, but are used when working with files containing binary data.

29.2 Understanding paths in C#

Paths in C# are represented by string values and will be formatted differently subject to the operating system type on which the code is running. On Windows systems, each path component is separated by a backslash (\) and is typically prefixed by a drive letter (C:\Users\Demo\Desktop). Systems that use the standard UNIX convention (macOS, Linux, iOS, Android, etc.) use the forward slash (/) to separate path components (/Users/Demo/Desktop).

When a program starts, the current working directory is the directory from which the app was launched. The current working directory of an application can be changed using the Directory and DirectoryInfo methods.

A filesystem top-level directory is referred to as the *root* directory and is represented by the '/' or' \' separator. Path names that begin with a '/' or '\' are said to be *absolute path names* in that they specify a filesystem location relative to the root directory. For example, "*/home/demo*" and "*C:\Temp\Files*" are absolute paths.

Paths that do not begin with a slash are interpreted to be *relative* to a current working directory. So, for example, if the current working directory is "C:*Users\Demo*" and the path is "*Documents\Letters*", then the path is considered to have an equivalent full, absolute pathname of "C:*Users\Demo\Documents\Letters*".

Windows-style paths present a problem because the backslash character represents escape sequences in C# strings. The following path, therefore, will cause a syntax error:

```
"C:\Users\Demo\Desktop\Profile.txt"
```

One option is to "escape" the backslash as follows:

```
"C:\\Users\\Demo\\Desktop\\Profile.txt"
```

Alternatively, Windows paths can be expressed as string literals:

```
@"C:\Users\Demo\Desktop\Profile.txt".
```

29.3 Creating the FileDemo project

Launch VS Code, open your "C# Essentials" workspace folder, and create a new .NET Console App project named FileDemo. Once the project is ready, open the *Program.cs* file and use it to try out the code examples in the rest of the chapter.

29.4 Current working directory

The initial current working directory of an app is the directory from which it was launched and can be identified using the Directory class. Edit the *Program.cs* file and use the static Directory.GetCurrentDirectory() method, as follows:

```
string currentDirectory = Directory.GetCurrentDirectory();
Console.WriteLine(currentDirectory);
```

Click the run button and check the terminal output where the current directory will be displayed. For example:

```
/Users/neilsmyth/Documents/Books/C#_13/C# Essentials/FileDemo
```

29.5 Checking if a directory exists

Both the Directory and DirectoryInfo classes provide a way to identify if a directory exists at a specified path. The following code checks for the existence of a directory named *MyFiles*. Note that since we are not prefixing the path with '/' or '\', the directory name is relative to the current working directory:

```
if (Directory.Exists("MyFiles"))
{
    Console.WriteLine("Directory Exists.");
}
else
{
    Console.WriteLine("Directory does not exist.");
}
```

The same result can be achieved by creating a DirectoryInfo instance initialized with the directory path and accessing the Exists property:

```
DirectoryInfo dirInfo = new("MyFiles");

if (dirInfo.Exists)
```

```
{
    Console.WriteLine("Directory Exists.");
}
else
{
    Console.WriteLine("Directory does not exist.");
}
```

29.6 Creating a Directory

Having identified that the directory does not exist, the next step is to create it. Directories are created in C# using the Directory.CreateDirectory() static method, or the Create() method of a DirectoryInfo object, for example:

```
if (Directory.Exists("MyFiles"))
{
    Console.WriteLine("Directory Exists.");
}
else
{
    Console.WriteLine("Directory does not exist - creating...");
    Directory.CreateDirectory("MyFiles");
}

DirectoryInfo dirInfo = new("MyFiles");

if (dirInfo.Exists)
{
    Console.WriteLine("Directory Exists.");
}
else
{
    Console.WriteLine("Directory does not exist - creating...");
    dirInfo.Create();
}
```

When the code runs, the first statement will detect that the directory does not exist and create it, the second statement will report that the directory now exists:

```
Directory does not exist - creating...
Directory Exists.
```

29.7 Deleting a Directory

Existing directories are deleted using the Delete() method of the Directory class, passing through as an argument the path of the directory to be deleted, for example:

```
Directory.Delete("/Temp/Images");
```

If the directory contains files or other sub-directories, the above method call will trigger an I/O exception indicating that the directory is not empty. To override this exception and delete the directory and all its files and subdirectories, pass it a Boolean true value as follows:

```
Directory.Delete("/Temp/Images", true);
```

29.8 Changing the current working directory

The current working directory can be changed by calling the Directory.SetCurrentDirectory() method and passing it the destination directory as an argument. As with all directory-related operations, the provided path can be absolute or relative. Add the following lines to the *Program.cs* file to change directory to the MyFiles folder:

```
Directory.SetCurrentDirectory("MyFiles");
Console.WriteLine(Directory.GetCurrentDirectory());
```

Run the code and confirm that the current directory has changed to the MyFiles subdirectory, for example:

```
/Users/neilsmyth/Dropbox/Documents/Books/C#_13/C# Essentials/FileDemo/MyFiles
```

29.9 Handling File and Directory Exceptions

When working with files and directories in C#, it is important to note that many operations have the potential to throw exceptions. Consider, for example, the above code to change the current working directory. The example works because we had checked for the existence of the MyFiles directory, and created it if necessary. The result, however, would have been different if the directory did not exist. To see this in action, add the following code to the project:

```
Directory.SetCurrentDirectory("MyFiles1");
```

Click the run button, at which point the program will terminate with the following unhandled DirectoryNotFoundException error:

```
Unhandled exception. System.IO.DirectoryNotFoundException: Could not find a part
of the path '/temp/MyFiles1'.
   at Interop.ThrowExceptionForIoErrno(ErrorInfo errorInfo, String path, Boolean
isDirError)
```

To avoid unhandled exceptions, file and directory handling must be coded defensively (for example checking a directory or file exists before referencing it) or performed within *try-catch* statements similar to the following:

```
try
{
    Directory.SetCurrentDirectory("MyFiles1");
}
catch (Exception ex)
{
    Console.WriteLine($"{ex.Message}");
}
```

29.10 File handling using the File class

With the basics of directory handling in C# covered, it is time to look at working with files. The System.IO File class provides a range of static methods for working with files, including creation, deletion, copying, reading, and writing. Equivalent methods are provided by the FileInfo class.

29.10.1 Checking if a file exists

As with directories, we can check for the presence of a file at a specified path by calling the File.Exists() method:

```
if (File.Exists("/tmp/MyFile.txt"))
{


}
```

29.10.2 Creating and opening files

We can also create and open files using the File.Open() method combined with a FileMode value:

```
var myFile = File.Open(<path>, FileMode.<mode>);
```

The following modes are available when opening files:

- **Append** - Opens the file if it exists, or creates a new one if it does not. Subsequent write operations are appended to the existing file content.
- **Create** - Creates a new file, or overwrites it if it already exists.
- **CreateNew** - Attempts to create a new file and throws an exception if the file already exists.
- **Open** - Opens an existing file and throws an exception if it doesn't exist.
- **OpenOrCreate** - If the file exists it is opened, otherwise a new file is created.
- **Truncate** - Opens an existing file and truncates it to zero length.

To create a new file, overwriting it if it already exists, we can use the following code:

```
File.Open("MyFile.txt", FileMode.Create);
```

29.10.3 Reading and writing using the File class

The WriteAllText() method writes a string to a specified file. If the file already exists, it will be overwritten with the new content, otherwise, a new file will be created.

Conversely, the ReadAllText() method will read the content of a specified file and return it as a string value. The following code writes a string to a file named *MyFile.txt* before reading it back:

```
File.WriteAllText("MyFile.txt", "Hello, this is some text.");

string content = File.ReadAllText("MyFile.txt");

Console.WriteLine($"content = {content}");
```

When the code executes, the following will appear in the terminal:

```
content = Hello, this is some text.
```

To append text to an existing file, we call the AppendAllText() method as follows:

```
File.WriteAllText("MyFile.txt", "Hello, this is some text.");
File.AppendAllText("MyFile.txt", " This is more text.");

string content = File.ReadAllText("MyFile.txt");

Console.WriteLine($"content = {content}");
```

The resulting terminal output will read as follows:

```
Hello, this is some text. This is more text.
```

To write multiple lines of text to a file in a single operation, place the lines in a list collection and pass it to the WriteAllLines() method:

```
List<string> textList = ["Kia Sorento", "Alfa Romeo GTV6", "Chevy Spark",
                         "Ford Explorer", "Toyota Celica"];
```

```
File.WriteAllLines("MyFile.txt", textList);
```

The ReadAllLines() method reads the entire content of a file and returns the lines of text as a string array:

```
string[] readList = File.ReadAllLines("MyFile.txt");

foreach (string line in readList) {
    Console.WriteLine(line);
}
```

Run the project and check for the following output in the terminal:

```
Kia Sorento
Alfa Romeo GTV6
Chevy Spark
Ford Explorer
Toyota Celica
```

29.11 Deleting, copying, and moving files

Existing files are deleted using the Delete() method of the File class (similar options are available in the FileInfo class), passing through the path of the file to be deleted, for example:

```
File.Delete("/Temp/SomeFile.txt");
```

To copy an existing file to a new file use the File.Copy() method as follows:

```
File.Copy("File1.txt", "/Temp/File2.txt");
```

The File.Move() method moves a file from one location to another, including the option to rename the file. The following code moves a file between directories:

```
File.Move("MyFile.txt", "/Documents/MyFile.txt");
```

In the following example, Move() is used to rename a file in the current working directory:

```
File.Move("oldfilename.txt", "newfilename.txt");
```

29.12 File I/O with streams

The File class provides a simple way to write content to files as blocks or lines of text. For more complex requirements, however, we need to use streams.

The StreamReader and StreamWriter classes are used to read from and write to files with greater flexibility and control compared to the File class and are also better suited for working with large files.

The Stream classes allow us to read and write text by line or character. The following code, for example, uses the StreamWriter Write() and WriteLine() methods to write individual characters and lines to the stream, respectively:

```
using (StreamWriter writer = new("MyFile.txt"))
{
    writer.Write('A');
    writer.Write('B');
    writer.Write('C');
    writer.WriteLine("DEFGHIJKLMNOP");
    writer.WriteLine("QRSTUVWXYZ");
}
```

Note the use of the *using* statement in the above code. StreamReader and StreamWriter allocate resources when they are created which need to be released when the work is complete. The *using* statement ensures the Dispose() method is called on the corresponding object on completion to free the allocated resources. Alternatively, the Dispose() must be called on the stream instance:

```
writer.Dispose();
```

The following code reads the content of the *MyFile.txt* file line by line using the StreamReader ReadLine() method:

```
using (StreamReader reader = new("MyFile.txt"))
{
    string line;

    while ((line = reader.ReadLine()) != null)
    {
        Console.WriteLine(line);
    }
}
```

We can use the StreamReader Read() method to read ranges of characters from a file. The Read() method has several overrides that allow it to be called in different ways. The following code, for example, reads and displays the first character from our *MyFile.txt* file:

```
Console.WriteLine($"Char = {(char)reader.Read()}");
```

Output:

```
Char = A
```

StreamReader instances retain a pointer indicating the current position in the file. The above code not only reads the first character from the file but also updates the pointer to reference the next position. A second read operation, therefore, would return the 'B' character.

To avoid the risk of reading beyond the end of a file, we can use the StreamReader Peek() method to see the next character without reading it. When Peek() returns -1 we know that the current character is the last:

```
while (reader.Peek() >= 0) {
    Console.WriteLine($"Char = {(char)reader.Read()}");
}
```

The Read() method, can also read a specified number of characters from a given index position using the following syntax:

```
Read(<char array>, <index>, <count>)
```

In the above syntax, the <index> parameter is an offset relative to the current stream position, not from the start of the stream. For example, if the stream pointer is currently 2 and Read() is passed an index value of 3, the characters will be read starting at position 5.

The following code example reads from the file in blocks of three characters, starting from the current position:

```
using (StreamReader reader = new("MyFile.txt"))
{
    char[] charBuffer;

    while (reader.Peek() >= 0)
```

```
    {
        charBuffer = new char[3];
        reader.Read(charBuffer, 0, 3);
        Console.WriteLine(charBuffer);
    }
}
```

When executed, the above code will generate the following output:

```
ABC
DEF
GHI
JKL
MNO
P
Q
RST
UVW
XYZ
```

The pattern is disrupted after the letter 'O', but keep in mind that this is where we switched from Write() to WriteLine(), which introduced a newline between the 'P' and 'Q'.

When working with streams, we can obtain the stream length by accessing the reader's BaseStream.Length property:

```
var length = reader.BaseStream.Length;
```

This is useful for initializing the character buffer when reading the entire stream:

```
char[] charBuffer;

var length = reader.BaseStream.Length;

while (reader.Peek() >= 0)
{
    charBuffer = new char[length];

    reader.Read(charBuffer, 0, (int)length);
    Console.WriteLine(charBuffer);
}
```

Another technique for reading until the end of the stream is to use the ReadToEnd() method, which returns a string value containing the stream's content from the current position to the end:

```
string contents = reader.ReadToEnd();
```

29.13 Asynchronous file handling

In addition to the synchronous methods covered so far, the File and Stream classes include asynchronous equivalents which are particularly helpful when working with large files. The following are some examples of these asynchronous methods:

- File.WriteAllLinesAsync()

- File.ReadAllLinesAsync()
- File.WriteAllTextAsync()
- File.ReadAllTextAsync()
- StreamReader.ReadAsync()
- StreamReader.ReadBlockAsync()
- StreamReader.ReadLineAsync()
- StreamReader.ReadToEndAsync()
- StreamWriter.WriteAsync()
- StreamWriter.WriteLineAsync()

These methods are syntactically similar to the synchronous equivalents but must be called from within async contexts using the await keyword, as outlined in the *"Asynchronous Programming in C#"* chapter.

29.14 Working with binary streams

So far in this chapter, we have worked exclusively with text-based files. For binary file handling, C# provides the BinaryReader and BinaryWriter classes. The following example writes string, boolean, double, integer, and char values to a binary file:

```
using (BinaryWriter writer = new(File.Open("Binary.dat", FileMode.Create)))
{
    writer.Write("Test data");
    writer.Write(false);
    writer.Write(3.57);
    writer.Write(33);
    writer.Write('W');
}
```

When reading from a binary stream, the appropriate BinaryReader method must be called to match the data type as follows:

```
using (BinaryReader reader = new(File.Open("Binary.dat", FileMode.Open)))
{
    Console.WriteLine("String = " + reader.ReadString());
    Console.WriteLine("Boolean = " + reader.ReadBoolean());
    Console.WriteLine("Double = " + reader.ReadDouble());
    Console.WriteLine("Int = " + reader.ReadInt32());
    Console.WriteLine("Char = " + reader.ReadChar());
}
```

When it runs, the above code will generate the following output:

```
String = Test data
Boolean = False
Double = 3.57
Int = 33
Char = W
```

29.15 Take the knowledge test

Click the link below or scan the QR code to test your knowledge and understanding of C# dictionary collections:

https://www.answertopia.com/65dc

29.16 Summary

This chapter explored file and directory handling in C# using classes from the System.IO namespace. We covered creating, deleting, navigating, and working with files and directories, including checking for existence, changing the current working directory, and handling exceptions. The File class provides static methods for working with files, while the FileInfo class offers non-static methods for the same purpose. We also looked at more complex file handling using the StreamReader, StreamWriter, BinaryReader, and BinaryWriter classes.

Chapter 30

30. C# Strings

Strings are collections of characters that are grouped together to form words or sentences. If it wasn't for humans, computers would probably never have anything to do with strings. The fact is, however, that one of the primary jobs of a computer is to accept data from and present data to humans. For this reason, it is highly likely that any C# program is going to involve a considerable amount of code specifically designed to work with data in the form of strings.

30.1 Creating the StringsDemo Project

Launch VS Code, open your "C# Essentials" workspace folder, and create a new .NET Console App project named StringsDemo.

After creating the project, open the *Program.cs* file and use it to try out the examples in the rest of this chapter.

30.2 Creating strings in C#

Strings consist of sequences of characters contained in a string object. A string object may be created using a number of different mechanisms.

A string may be declared but not initialized as follows:

```
string myString;
```

Alternatively, you can assign a literal value to a string in C# using the assignment operator:

```
string myString = "Hello World";
```

It is, of course, also possible to declare a string using implicit typing:

```
var myString = "Hello World";
```

Similarly, a new string may be created using the new keyword and passing through the literal value to the constructor:

```
string myString = new("Hello World");
```

String literals are placed within double quotes (as shown above). If the string itself contains double quotes, the escape character (\) should precede the double-quote characters:

```
Console.WriteLine("He shouted \"Can you hear me?\"");
```

Output:

```
He shouted "Can you hear me?"
```

You can also instruct C# to treat all the characters in a string verbatim by prefixing the string with the @ character. When using @ notation, everything between the double quotes is treated as a raw string, regardless of whether new lines, carriage returns, backslashes, etc., are present in the text. For example:

```
Console.WriteLine(@"You can put a backslash \ here
and a new line
and tabs                work too.
You can also put in sequences that would normally be seen as escape sequences 
like \n and \t.");
```

Output:

```
You can put a backslash \ here
and a new line
and tabs                  work too.
You can also put in sequences that would normally be seen as escape sequences
like \n and \t.
```

If you are familiar with the heredoc function of other programming languages, you will quickly notice that this is essentially the C# equivalent.

30.3 Obtaining the length of a C# string

If you need to identify the length of a C# string, you can do so by accessing the Length property of the string object:

```
string myString = "Hello World";
Console.WriteLine($"myString length = {myString.Length}");
```

Output:

```
myString length = 11
```

30.4 Treating strings as arrays

It is possible to access individual characters in a string by treating the string as an array (arrays were covered in *"Creating 2D, 3D, and Jagged Arrays in C#"*).

By specifying the index value using subscripting syntax ([]), you can access individual characters in a string (keeping in mind that the first character is at index position 0):

```
string myString = "Hello World";

Console.WriteLine(myString[0]);
Console.WriteLine(myString[2]);
Console.WriteLine(myString[4]);
```

Output:

```
H
l
o
```

It is important to note that strings are immutable (in other words, while an entirely new string literal may be assigned to the variable, you cannot change the individual characters in a string). To experience this limitation, try running the following code:

```
string myString = "Hello World";

myString[5] = '-';
```

When attempting to run the above code, you will have received an error from the compiler stating the following:

```
Property or indexer 'string.this[int]' cannot be assigned to -- it is read only
```

It is also possible to convert a string to an array of characters by making a call to the string object's ToCharArray() method as follows:

```
string myString = "Hello World";
```

```
char[] charArray = myString.ToCharArray();

foreach (char c in charArray) {
    Console.WriteLine(c);
}
```

Output:

```
H
e
l
l
o

W
o
r
l
d
```

30.5 String character iteration

Given that we can treat each character in an array as an array element, it should not surprise you to learn that we can iterate through the characters of a string using a *foreach* loop as follows:

```
string myString = "Hello World";

foreach (char c in myString) {
    Console.WriteLine(c);
}
```

Output:

```
G
o
o
d
b
y
e

W
o
r
l
d
```

30.6 Concatenating strings

Strings may be concatenated (i.e., joined together) simply by adding them together using the addition operator (+).

We can, therefore, combine two strings as follows:

```
string myString = "Hello World.";

Console.WriteLine(myString + " How are you?");
```

Output:

```
Hello World. How are you?
```

Alternatively, you can concatenate strings using the Concat() instance method of the string class. This method takes two strings to be joined as arguments and returns a new string containing the union of the two strings:

```
string myString1 = "If at first you don't succeed, ";
string myString2 = "try, try again.";

string myString3 = string.Concat(myString1, myString2);

Console.WriteLine(myString3);
```

Output:

```
If at first you don't succeed, try, try again.
```

30.7 Comparing strings

C# provides several options if you need to compare one string with another. The most common option is to use the equality operator, as demonstrated in the example below:

```
string myString1 = "Hello World";
string myString2 = "Hello World";

if (myString1 == myString2)
{
    Console.WriteLine("The strings match.");
}
else
{
    Console.WriteLine("They strings not match.");
}
```

Output:

```
The strings match
```

You can also compare strings in a similar way using the string.Equals() instance method. This method takes as arguments two strings to be compared and returns a Boolean result indicating whether or not the strings match:

```
string myString1 = "Hello world";
string myString2 = "Hello world";

if (string.Equals(myString1, myString2))
{
    Console.WriteLine("The strings match.");
}
else
{
```

```
    Console.WriteLine("The strings do not match.");
}
```

Output:

```
The strings match.
```

In the above example, we passed both strings through to the Equals() method when performing the comparison. The Equals() method can also be called on a string literal or string object to achieve the same result:

```
string myString1 = "Hello world";
string myString2 = "Hello world";

if (myString1.Equals(myString2, StringComparison.Ordinal))
{
    Console.WriteLine("The strings match.");
}
else
{
    Console.WriteLine("The strings do not match.");
}
```

Output:

```
The strings match.
```

So far, all of the comparisons we have explored have performed a case-sensitive comparison. When calling the Equals() method, you can also pass through a comparison type parameter. The type must be taken from the C# StringComparison enumeration, which, among values for performing culture-sensitive comparison settings, includes the OrdinalIgnoreCase value for case-insensitive comparisons:

```
string myString1 = "HELLO WORLD";
string myString2 = "Hello world";

if (string.Equals(myString1, myString2, StringComparison.OrdinalIgnoreCase))
{
    Console.WriteLine("The strings match.");
}
else
{
    Console.WriteLine("The strings do not match.");
}
```

Output:

```
The strings match.
```

The same approach also works when calling the Equals() method directly on a string literal or object:

```
var result = "My String".Equals("my string", StringComparison.OrdinalIgnoreCase);
```

The string.Compare() method provides yet another way to compare strings, though this method has some useful additional features. This method accepts as arguments the two strings to be compared and returns an integer value indicating how the strings relate to each other in relation to sort order. A result of 0 indicates that the strings match. A value of less than 0 indicates that the first string precedes the second string in the sort order. Finally, a result of greater than 0 indicates the second string precedes the first in the sort order:

```
string myString1 = "Bananas are yellow.";
string myString2 = "Oranges are orange.";

var result = string.Compare(myString1, myString2);

if (result == 0)
{
    Console.WriteLine("Strings match.");
}
else if (result < 0)
{
    Console.WriteLine("myString1 precedes myString2 in sort order.");
}
else if (result > 0)
{
    Console.WriteLine("myString2 precedes myString1 in sort order.");
}
```

Output:

```
myString1 precedes myString2 in sort order.
```

30.8 Changing string case

The case of the characters in a string may be changed using the ToUpper() and ToLower() methods. Both of these methods return a modified string rather than changing the actual string. For example:

```
string myString = "Hello World";
string newString;

newString = myString.ToUpper();
Console.WriteLine(newString);

newString = myString.ToLower();
Console.WriteLine(newString);
```

Output:

```
HELLO WORLD
hello world
```

30.9 Splitting a string into multiple parts

A string may be separated into multiple parts using the Split() method. Split() takes as an argument the character to use as the delimiter to identify the points at which the string is to be split. Returned from the method call is an array containing the individual parts of the string. For example, the following code splits a string up using the comma character as the delimiter. The results are placed in an array called myColors and a *foreach* loop then reads each item from the array and displays it:

```
string myString = "Red, Green, Blue, Yellow, Pink, Purple";
string[] myColors = myString.Split(',');

foreach (string color in myColors)
```

```
{
    Console.WriteLine(color);
}
```

Output:

```
Red Green Blue Yellow Pink Purple
```

As we can see, the Split() method broke the string up as requested, but we have a problem in that the spaces are still present. Fortunately, C# provides a method to handle this.

30.10 Trimming and padding strings

Unwanted leading and trailing spaces can be removed from a string using the Trim() method. When called, this method returns a modified version of the string with both leading and trailing spaces removed:

```
string myString = "    hello      ";

Console.WriteLine("[" + myString + "]");
Console.WriteLine("[" + myString.Trim() + "]");
```

Output:

```
[    hello      ]
[hello]
```

If you only need to remove leading or trailing spaces, use either the TrimStart() or TrimEnd() method respectively.

The inverse of the trim methods are the PadLeft() and PadRight() methods. These methods allow leading or trailing characters to be added to a string. The methods take as arguments the total number of characters to which the string is to be padded and the padding character:

```
string myString = "hello";

string newString;
newString = myString.PadLeft(10, ' ');
newString = newString.PadRight(20, '*');
Console.WriteLine("[" + newString + "]");
```

Output:

```
[     hello**********]
```

30.11 String replacement

Parts of a string may be replaced using the Replace() method. This method takes the part of the string to be replaced and the replacement string as arguments and returns a new string reflecting the change. The Replace() method will replace all instances of the string:

```
string myString = "Hello World";
string newString;

Console.WriteLine(myString);
newString = myString.Replace("Hello", "Goodbye");
Console.WriteLine(newString);
```

Output:

```
Hello World
```

```
Goodbye World
```

30.12 Take the knowledge test

Click the link below or scan the QR code to test your knowledge and understanding of C# strings:

https://www.answertopia.com/nppx

30.13 Summary

C# strings are collections of characters used for human-computer interaction. Strings can be created using literals, new keyword, or implicit typing. They can be manipulated using methods like Length(), ToCharArray(), and Concat(), and iterated over using *foreach* loops.

C# provides various methods for comparing strings, including equality operators like Equals(), and Compare(). The ToUpper() and ToLower() methods can change string case, while Split() separates strings into parts. Trim() removes leading and trailing spaces, while PadLeft() and PadRight() add characters to the beginning or end of a string.

Chapter 31

31. C# String Formatting

In addition to the wide selection of string manipulation functions outlined in the previous chapter, the string class also provides the Format() method.

The primary purpose of the C# string Format() method is to provide a way of inserting string, numerical, or boolean values into a string with additional formatting control.

31.1 The Syntax of the string Format() method

The general syntax of the string Format() method is as follows:

```
string.Format("format string", arg1, arg2, .... );
```

The format string is the string into which the values will be placed. Within this string are placeholders that indicate the location of each value within the string. Placeholders take the form of braces {} surrounding a number indicating the corresponding argument to be substituted for the placeholder. Following on from the format string is a comma-separated list of arguments. There must be an argument for each of the placeholders.

31.2 Creating the StringFormatDemo project

Launch VS Code, open your "C# Essentials" workspace folder, and create a new .NET Console App project named StringFormatDemo.

After creating the project, open the *Program.cs* file and use it to try out the examples in the rest of this chapter.

31.3 A simple string formatting example

The following code example demonstrates a straightforward use of the string Format() method:

```
string newString;

newString = string.Format("There are {0} cats in my {1} and no {2}", 2, "house", 
"dogs");
Console.WriteLine (newString);
```

Output:

```
There are 2 cats in my house and no dogs
```

Let"s quickly review the string Format() method call in the above example. The format string contains three placeholders indicated by {0}, {1}, and {2}. Following the format string are the arguments to be used in each placeholder. So, for example, {0} is replaced by the first argument (the number 2), the {1} by the second argument (the string "house"), and so on.

If you cast your mind back to the *"C# Variables and Constants"* chapter, you will probably wonder how this compares to the string interpolation technique we have used countless times throughout the book. As we will see below, C# string formatting becomes more useful when combined with format controls.

31.4 Using format controls

So far, we have only substituted arguments for placeholders, but we have not changed the format of the arguments before they are displayed. This essentially instructs the Format() method to use the default formatting for each argument type when displaying the string. Perhaps the most powerful aspect of the Format() method is the ability to use format controls within the placeholders to control the output format.

Format controls appear inside the braces ({}) of the placeholders. The format of a placeholder with a format control is as follows:

```
{n:controlx}
```

In the above syntax, *n* is the placeholder number and *control* is the special format control sequence to be applied to the argument. The *x* optional number further formats the output for certain control types.

31.5 A simple format control example

The following example uses the X format control, which is used to display a number using hexadecimal format:

```
var newString = string.Format("The number {0} in Hexadecimal is {0:X}.", 432);

Console.WriteLine (newString);
```

Output:

```
The number 432 in Hexadecimal is 1B0.
```

The above example displays argument 0 (432) in two formats. The first is the default decimal format, while the second uses the X format control to display the argument as a hexadecimal number.

The string Format() method provides a wide range of format controls which we will explore below.

31.6 C# string Format() format controls

The following table lists format controls supported by the C# string Format() method together with examples of each control:

Control	Type	Description	Example
C	Currency	Displays number prefixed with the currency symbol appropriate to the current locale	{0:C} of 432.00 outputs $432.00
D	Decimal	Displays numbers in decimal form with optional padding	{0:D4} of 432 outputs 00432
E	Exponential	Displays number in scientific form with optional value for the fractional part	{0:E5} of 432.32 outputs 4.32320E+002
F	Fixed	Displays the number, including the specified number of decimal digits	{0:F3} of 432.324343 outputs 432.324
N	Number	Converts a number to a human-friendly format by inserting commas and rounding to the nearest 100th	{0:N} of 123432.324343 outputs 123,432.32
X	Hexadecimal	Converts a number to hexadecimal	{0:X} of 432 outputs 1B0
0:0...	Zero Padding	Adds zeros to pad argument	{0:0000.00} of 43.1 outputs 0043.10
0:0#...	Space Padding	Adds spaces to pad argument	{0:####.##} of 43.1 outputs 43.1
%	Percentage	Multiplies the argument by 100 and appends a percentage sign	{0:00.00%} of .432 outputs 43.20%

Table 31-1

Before moving on to the next chapter, run the following code to see some of these format controls in action:

```
var newString = string.Format("The number {0} fixed to 2 decimal places is
{0:F2}.", 109.78799);

Console.WriteLine (newString);

newString = string.Format("The number {0} using human friendly formatting is
{0:N}.", 1023429.78799);
Console.WriteLine (newString);
newString = string.Format("The number {0} using exponential formatting is
{0:E6}.", 32423.24232);
Console.WriteLine (newString);

newString = string.Format("The number {0} as a percentage to 3 decinal places is
{0:00.000%}.", 0.24232);
Console.WriteLine (newString);
```

Output:

```
The number 109.78799 fixed to 2 decimal places is 109.79.
The number 1023429.78799 using human friendly formatting is 1,023,429.79.
The number 32423.24232 using exponential formatting is 3.242324E+004.
The number 0.24232 as a percentage to 3 decinal places is 24.232%.
```

31.7 Take the knowledge test

Click the link below or scan the QR code to test your knowledge and understanding of C# string formatting:

https://www.answertopia.com/yywc

31.8 Summary

The C# string Format() method allows for inserting values into a string with formatting control. Format controls, such as C for currency and X for hexadecimal, can be used within placeholders to modify the output format. The method provides a wide range of format controls for various data types.

Chapter 32

32. C# Dates and Times

It is a rare application that can be developed without in some way needing to work with dates and times. Recognizing this, the Microsoft engineers responsible for C# gave us the DateTime object. This chapter will look at using this object to work with dates and times in C# based applications. Topics covered include adding and subtracting time, getting the system date and time, and formatting and extracting elements of dates and times in C#.

32.1 Creating the DateTimeDemo project

Launch VS Code, open your "C# Essentials" workspace folder, and create a new .NET Console App project named DateTimeDemo.

After creating the project, open the *Program.cs* file and use it to try out the examples in the rest of this chapter.

32.2 Creating a C# DateTime object

The first step in using the DateTime object when working with dates and times in C# is to create an object instance. You do this using the *new* keyword passing through year, month, and day values. For example, to create a DateTime object preset to April 9, 2024, you would write the following code:

```
DateTime meetingAppt = new(2024, 4, 9);
Console.WriteLine (meetingAppt.ToString());
```

Output:

```
4/9/2024 12:00:00 AM
```

In the above example, after setting the date, we use the ToString() method of the DateTime object to output the current date and time value as a string.

Note that if a time is not specified along with the date, the DateTime class constructor will set the time to 12:00 am.

Time values are specified by passing through hours, minutes, and seconds values to the constructor. The following code, for example, sets the time property of a DateTime object to 14:30:00 using the same date as before:

```
DateTime meetingAppt = new(2024, 4, 9, 14, 30, 0);
Console.WriteLine (meetingAppt.ToString());
```

Output:

```
4/9/2024 2:30:00 PM
```

32.3 Getting the current system time and date

The system date and time of the computer on which the C# code is executing may be accessed using the Today and Now static properties of the DateTime class. The Today property will return the current system date (and the time set to 12:00 AM), while the Now property returns the current date and time. For example, the following code demonstrates these properties (keeping in mind that the server on which the code is executing may not be in your timezone):

```
Console.WriteLine(DateTime.Today.ToString());
Console.WriteLine(DateTime.Now.ToString());
```

Output:

```
8/16/2024 12:00:00 AM
8/16/2024 10:32:37 AM
```

32.4 Adding to or subtracting from dates and times

The C# DateTime object provides several methods for adding or subtracting dates and times from a DateTime object instance. These methods are outlined in the following table:

Method	Description
Add	Adds/Subtracts the value of the specified TimeSpan object instance.
AddDays	Adds/Subtracts the specified number of days.
AddHours	Adds/Subtracts the specified number of hours.
AddMilliseconds	Adds/Subtracts the specified number of Milliseconds.
AddMinutes	Adds/Subtracts the specified number of minutes.
AddMonths	Adds/Subtracts the specified number of months.
AddSeconds	Adds/Subtracts the specified number of seconds.
AddYears	Adds/Subtracts the specified number of years.

Table 32-1

A vital issue to understand is that these methods do not change the value of the DateTime object on which the method is called but instead return a new DateTime object primed with the modified date and time. For example, add five days to our example as follows:

```
DateTime meetingAppt = new(2024, 4, 9, 14, 30, 0);
DateTime newAppt = meetingAppt.AddDays(5);
Console.WriteLine(newAppt.ToString());
```

Output:

```
4/14/2024 2:30:00 PM
```

To subtract from a date and time, pass through a negative value to the appropriate method. For example, we can subtract ten months from our example object as follows:

```
DateTime meetingAppt = new(2024, 4, 9, 14, 30, 0);
DateTime newAppt = meetingAppt.AddMonths(-10);
Console.WriteLine(newAppt.ToString());
```

Output:

```
6/9/2023 2:30:00 PM
```

32.5 Retrieving parts of a date and time

Dates and times comprise distinct and separate values, namely the day, month, year, hours, minutes, seconds, and milliseconds. The C# DateTime object stores each value as a separate property within the object, allowing each to be accessed individually. For example, the following code sample extracts each value and displays it in the console:

```
DateTime meetingAppt = new(2024, 4, 9, 14, 30, 0);

Console.WriteLine(meetingAppt.Day);
Console.WriteLine(meetingAppt.Month);
```

```
Console.WriteLine(meetingAppt.Year);
Console.WriteLine(meetingAppt.Hour);
Console.WriteLine(meetingAppt.Minute);
Console.WriteLine(meetingAppt.Second);
Console.WriteLine(meetingAppt.Millisecond);
```

Output:

```
9
4
2023
14
30
0
0
```

32.6 Take the knowledge test

Click the link below or scan the QR code to test your knowledge and understanding of C# Dates and Times:

https://www.answertopia.com/ants

32.7 Summary

In this chapter, we learned about the C# DateTime object, which is used for handling dates and times in C# applications. We discussed how to create a DateTime object by specifying a date or by including time values. We also looked at how to access the current date and time using the Today and Now properties. Additionally, we explored the various methods provided by the DateTime object for manipulating dates and times, such as adding or subtracting days, months, years, and other time units. Finally, we covered how to extract individual components like the day, month, year, hour, and minute using DateTime properties, which allows for working with specific elements of dates and times.

Index

Symbols

A

B

E

F

G

H

I

J

L

M

T

www.ingramcontent.com/pod-product-compliance
Lightning Source LLC
LaVergne TN
LVHW080115070326
832902LV00015B/2601

* 9 7 8 1 9 6 5 7 6 4 0 2 2 *